The Alignment of
Foreign Exchange Rates

Fritz Machlup

The Praeger Special Studies program—utilizing the most modern and efficient book production techniques and a selective worldwide distribution network—makes available to the academic, government, and business communities significant, timely research in U.S. and international economic, social, and political development.

The Alignment of Foreign Exchange Rates
The First Horowitz Lectures

PRAEGER SPECIAL STUDIES IN INTERNATIONAL ECONOMICS AND DEVELOPMENT

Praeger Publishers   New York   Washington   London

PRAEGER PUBLISHERS
111 Fourth Avenue, New York, N.Y. 10003, U.S.A.
5, Cromwell Place, London S.W.7, England

Published in the United States of America in 1972
by Praeger Publishers, Inc.

Library of Congress Catalog Card Number: 72-169260

Printed in the United States of America

On the occasion of the seventieth birthday of David Horowitz, first Governor of the Bank of Israel, the Israel Banks' Association and the Eliezer Kaplan School of Economics and Social Sciences of the Hebrew University of Jerusalem jointly established a series of annual Horowitz Lectures on Money and International Finance. Each series is delivered in two parts; one lecture is given in Jerusalem and the second in Tel Aviv.

This volume contains the first series of the Horowitz Lectures, delivered in January 1970.

PREFACE

The theme and main thesis of my two lectures may be stated in the following proposition: When past or ongoing events have produced or are producing an imbalance of international payments that is not almost certain to be corrected or reversed shortly by developments known to be under way, the best option available, under conditions usually prevailing in most countries, is a realignment of foreign-exchange rates.

In the first lecture I shall analyze alternative options for restoring balance and attempt to evaluate their comparative costs and advantages, presenting thereby the arguments that support my thesis.

In the second lecture I shall deal with the problem of timing, that is, with the question of the promptness with which the realignment of exchange rates should be undertaken if the costs to society are to be made as low as possible.

CONTENTS

The Alignment of
Foreign Exchange Rates

Those who know my expository style will expect me to begin with a few terminological remarks. I will not disappoint them. But you may find it helpful to have at the start a brief outline of the whole lecture.

I shall first discuss how the terms alignment and disalignment are related to the more usual terms equilibrium and disequilibrium and, particularly, to the expression "equilibrium exchange rates." I shall then address myself to the twin questions, how exchange rates get out of line and how imbalances can be redressed. The second of these questions will cause me to return to an old theme of mine: the difference between the use of selective correctives and of general adjustment policies that operate on relative levels of prices, costs, and incomes. Elaborating on this issue, I shall examine how supply and demand can be adjusted to a given exchange rate and how the exchange rate can be adjusted to supply and demand. Digressing from the main theme, I shall discuss the combination of monetary and fiscal policies, attempt to clarify some obscurities in the theory of the policy mix, and contrast international with interprovincial adjustment. Then we ought to be ready for the main task, the comparison of the cost of alternative policies. We shall find that exchange-rate adjustment is socially less costly than its alternatives and that, although all adjustment, regardless of the technique chosen, is painful, nonadjustment or postponed adjustment may eventually be even more painful and, in the meanwhile, will have caused severe damage to the economy.

ALIGNMENT AND EQUILIBRIUM

I speak of alignment and realignment of the exchange rate although most economists prefer to use other terms. The most favored terminology refers to the "equilibrium exchange rate," an expression which is often misleading. Even the simple reference to "equilibrium" is usually out of place. Many years ago I published a paper with the title "Equilibrium and Disequilibrium: Misplaced Concreteness and Disguised Politics," warning against the common misuse of these terms.[1]

Equilibrium and Disequilibrium

Equilibrium is quite often used for, or confused with, *stability of the price level*. Remember, however, that a rise in the price level may be the adjustment (equilibration) necessitated by certain events, measures, or developments: for example, demand inflation abroad may have led to a relative undervaluation of the currency if fixed exchange rates are maintained, resulting in an excess supply of foreign currencies, a surplus in the balance of payments, that will last until the domestic price level is sufficiently pulled up by the "imported inflation."

Equilibrium is often used for *full employment*. Remember, however, that the emergence or increase of unemployment may become necessary in the process of adjustment (equilibration) engineered by monetary restraint designed to reduce effective demand enough to allow the maintenance of an exchange rate that has overvalued the currency.

Equilibrium is sometimes used as the *opposite of disequilibrium*. Remember, however, that a situation may be both equilibrium and disequilibrium at the same time, depending on the length of the time horizon and on the precise set of variables admitted to the system.

Equilibrium is often used to denote something "good," a *desirable state*, a satisfactory situation. Remember, however, that most measures of economic policy are designed to alter an undesirable state, that is, to disturb an equilibrium that is regarded as unsatisfactory.

Conscious of these and other misunderstandings, one had better leave the term to those engaged in purely theoretical arguments far from any practical-political applications.

The Equilibrium Exchange Rate

Admittedly, the expression "equilibrium exchange rate" has been used even by writers who were well aware and not guilty of the confusions just enumerated. They evidently meant to refer to the exchange rate at which the amount of a currency supplied in the foreign-exchange market was—without any official intervention—equal to the amount demanded, given all the conditions that were prevailing and were continuing to prevail. Among these conditions determining the supply and the demand in the foreign-exchange market were interest rates, profit rates, wage rates, and scores of other variables. Why then single out the exchange rates from the set of variables? Why not speak of equilibrium interest rates, equilibrium profit rates, equilibrium price levels, or equilibrium wage rates, instead of equilibrium exchange rates? If all the variables in a system have precisely the values or magnitudes to make them consistent with one another, so that there is no inherent tendency for any of them to change, what sense does it make to single out one of the variables and declare that it is at an equilibrium level or of an equilibrium size?

Perhaps we can discover a reason for the seemingly arbitrary choice: All other variables are more difficult to influence in a predetermined way, let alone to move to a particular height or to change to a particular size, than the exchange rate. There is surely no easy way to adjust wage rates, either the structure or the level of wages, if they should be out of kilter with other relevant variables.

Commodity prices, especially the prices of goods traded in competitive markets, cannot be manipulated either, except in very indirect ways and with rather uncertain success. Effective demand and aggregate income can be controlled somewhat more dependably, though by no means directly, but the side effects and repercussions are sometimes unforeseeable and usually quite undesirable. Interest rates can be manipulated to some extent, but the effects on international movements of capital and on domestic investment and business activity make the long-run consequences of such manipulations rather uncertain and sometimes even the opposite of what is intended. Compared with all these attempts at equilibration, the foreign-exchange rate may appear as the variable that can be adjusted most directly and with more foreseeable results. This theoretical difference may have persuaded some economists to accept the terminological partiality toward one of many variables and confer upon it the title "equilibrium exchange rate."

Many who attempt to apply theoretical models to historical instances fail to notice the wide gulf between concrete situations of the real world and hypothetical situations in abstract theorizing. The idea of an exchange rate that will equilibrate supply and demand in the foreign-exchange market in the long run without changes in monetary reserves *as long as the conditions that determine supply and demand remain unchanged* has been confused with the idea of unchanged monetary reserves over a number of years while conditions change, as they are liable to change in reality.

In order to eliminate the effects of seasonal and cyclical changes, the late Ragnar Nurkse proposed a ten-year period as the real-world equivalent of the theoretical long run and stated that an exchange rate that had allowed the volume of monetary reserves to be the same as it was ten years earlier would have been an equilibrium exchange rate. This proposition lacked the theorist's traditional reservation of "other things being unchanged," the *ceteris paribus* clause. It thus left open whether in reality nothing of any significance had changed, or whether by sheer coincidence several offsetting changes had conspired to bring monetary reserves back to the size they had been ten years earlier or, thirdly, whether the authorities through clever use of monetary, fiscal, commercial, and other policies had contrived to fix things up to get interest rates, profit rates, wage rates, commodity prices, employment, total income, and what not, to precisely those values that would be compatible with unchanged exchange rates. If these three interpretations are left open, the concept of the equilibrium exchange rate becomes worthless for purposes of analysis and even for purposes of communication.

Disequilibrium Exchange Rates

If equilibrium is understood as mutual consistency or compatibility of all of a selected set of variables in an abstract theoretical model, then the concept is theoretically significant and may also be relevant for explanations of real-world situations, though only as an analogy. The concept, correctly understood, helps in making it clear that in a world in which things change all the time it must be extremely unlikely for any variable to have its equilibrium value unchanged from one month to another. We know that labor force, employment, production, productivity, incomes, money supply, velocity of circulation, interest rates, investment, profits, international flows of capital, and many other relevant economic quantities change all the time, and some quite considerably. Since exchange rates always refer to pairs of different currencies, and since each is linked through cross rates to all other currencies, and since changes go on in all countries, it would be a miracle if the exchange rate of a currency, if it is held constant, were to remain fully consistent with all other variables. It can be held constant through interventions in the exchange markets, that is, through sales and purchases of foreign currencies by the monetary authorities.

These official interventions allow "disequilibrium exchange rates" to be maintained for considerable periods. When imbalances become too great or too protracted, the authorities may be compelled to consider realignment of the exchange rate. But such realignment will rarely mean that the new rate will be fixed at the new "equilibrium level." If reserves have become almost depleted during years in which the currency was overvalued, the authorities will be inclined to fix a rate at which reserves can again be built up, that is, they will fix a rate that undervalues the currency. Thus, they will move from one disequilibrium position to another, from an overvaluation to an undervaluation. In the opposite situation, if a realignment is made in order to stop a flood of foreign currencies flowing into monetary reserves and to slow down the inflation thereby imported, the authorities may be inclined to leave some slight undervaluation to be removed by the price and income changes already initiated through the surplus of foreign payments. Again, therefore, alignment of the exchange rate need not mean bringing it to what is thought to be the equilibrium level at the moment.

Quite apart, however, from official decisions regarding realignment, the point to bear in mind is that foreign-exchange rates kept unchanged in a system of official intervention in the market are more often disequilibrium rates than equilibrium rates. The question is only how far out of line they are. If the disalignment is big or if it continues for a long time, it will be called a "fundamental disequilibrium" under the terms of the Articles of Agreement which established the International Monetary Fund.

HOW EXCHANGE RATES GET OUT OF LINE

Any change of any of the many relevant variables, at home or abroad, may cause a given foreign-exchange rate to become disaligned to some extent. It has long been the custom among monetary experts to distinguish structural and monetary changes. In old books authors spoke of changes "on the side of goods" and changes "on the side of money"; more recently the distinction has been between the "supply of goods and services" and, on the other side, the "effective demand" by those who have money to spend or are able to obtain it.

Causes of Disalignment

Experts have usually been agreed in the judgment that severe disalignments of exchange rates were, as a rule, the result of monetary causes. Changes on the supply side, it has been thought, were only relatively small and gradual and thus could not normally account for significant disalignments of exchange rates, especially since several of these changes would be unlikely to pull in the same direction; they would more likely offset one another in their effects on international flows of goods, services, and capital. However, small effects may cumulate to large totals over the years: If net effects within a year were as little as between 1 and 2 per cent in terms of over- or undervaluation of the currency at a fixed exchange rate, but net effects in subsequent years happened to be in the same direction, the disalignment of the fixed rate could after four years be as much as 7 or 8 per cent. This would mean, if the rate is maintained, heavy losses of monetary reserves, imposing on the country a choice of deflation and unemployment or of restrictions on trade and capital flows, and in the opposite case heavy accruals to monetary reserves, imposing on the country price inflation and sacrifices of consumption and domestic investment.

The polar distinction between structural and monetary factors causing disalignments of exchange rates does not convey an adequate idea of the forces that may be at work. Classifying is usually a rather arbitrary business, but the following grouping into more categories and subcategories may allow a better understanding of the possible "concatenation of circumstances" (to use the upper-high-brow expression favored in institutional economics). Let us note again that several of the disaligning forces may be offset by others pulling in the opposite direction. Many observers count on the offsets so confidently that they underrate the probability of net effects producing disalignment.

The classification which I propose turns on differences between countries and changes within countries; the differences relate either to rates of increase in magnitudes that have upward trends in almost all countries or to behavior functions, expressed as ratios between magnitudes (coefficients, propensities), that are assumed to be relatively stable over time.

1. *Differences in (annual) rates of increase of*   —⟶ interest rate

    1.1 effective demand, or (going back to some of the determinants of its change),

        1.11 the supply of domestic money,

        1.12 the private demand for domestic money (to hold), and

          1.13 the private demand for foreign-currency holdings;

1.2   real national product, or (going back to some of the determinants of its change),
      1.21 the labor force and its rate of employment,
      1.22 the capital stock and its utilization, and
      1.23 factor productivity (efficiency);

1.3   wage rates and commodity prices, or (more specifically)
      1.31 wage rates,
      1.32 commodity-price level in general, or
      1.33 prices in export industries and in industries competing with imports.

2.   *Differences in, and changes of, marginal and average propensities*

    2.1   to import,
    2.2   to save, and
    2.3   to consume exportable products.

3.   *Changes in*

    3.1   supply and demand of goods and services, especially in
       3.11 the composition of demand,
       3.12 comparative cost conditions,
       3.13 taxation and tax incidence,
       3.14 tariffs and other trade restrictions;

    3.2   capital movements and other financial transfers, or specifically,
       3.21 flows of long-term capital,
       3.22 flows of short-term capital,
       3.23 unilateral transfers, including grants to and from foreign countries and military expenditures in or by foreign countries.

The Conjuncture of Forces

In a large number of countries, no doubt, the repeated disalignments of exchange rates (despite frequent changes designed as

realignments) can be adequately explained by money inflation (1.11)
associated with wage and price inflations (1.3), and none of the other
causes needs to be exhibited. However, if one were to confine oneself
to these two factors, a very incomplete picture would be obtained of
several countries that have had only creeping inflations. It is well
understood that a country with a faster increase in money supply
need not get its payments balance into deficit if also the demand for
money (1.12) and the real national product (1.2) increase faster than
in other countries. We know, moreover, that a faster increase in
effective demand (1.1) associated with a faster increase in the general
wage and price levels (1.3) may be consistent with a payments
surplus if prices in export industries (1.33) rise much less than the
general price level, if the marginal propensity to import (2.1) is
lower, if comparative-cost conditions (3.12) change so as to make
several industries more competitive, or if more capital or other
financial transfers (3.2) are received from abroad.

In recent years much of the discussion of exchange-rate
disalignment has concentrated on differential rates of price increase
(1.32). This may be perfectly adequate in many instances, but is
surely insufficient in some important ones. Where the countries
compared have wide-open economies, differences in the increase of
effective demand (1.1) need not be reflected in differences in the
rates of price increase; the deficit-creating effects of a larger demand
inflation, even where it is not reflected in higher prices, may be
further aggravated by high propensities to import (2.1). And, of
course, the effects of capital movements (3.2) may always offset or
reinforce whatever other forces have been operative.

One novel point has recently impressed many students of this
subject. Even if a country has had practically the same rates of increase
of effective demand, real national product, wage rates, and commodity
prices, as its trading partners, a deviation of its marginal propensity to
import from those of other countries will produce an imbalance—a payments deficit if its import propensity is higher, and a surplus if it is
lower. It happens that the income elasticity of demand for imports is
especially high in some countries, including the United States, and
especially low in other countries, including Japan. This should not induce us to rely on this one point for full explanations of the con-
spicuous disalignment of the exchange rates of the U.S. dollar and
the yen, but the point is probably of considerable importance.

HOW IMBALANCES CAN BE REDRESSED

In discussing the question how imbalances can be redressed one does not have to make a distinction between partial and full redress. The techniques are the same, and whether they will remove or merely reduce an existing imbalance depends only on the degree of their application.

If one rules out segmenting the market by explicit or implicit application of multiple exchange rates, there are in principle only two ways of dealing with an imbalance in the foreign-exchange market: either to adjust supply and demand to the exchange rate or to adjust the exchange rate to supply and demand.

Segmentation of the market, however, is usually not ruled out; on the contrary, it is the first thing that occurs to governments, legislators, politicians, bureaucrats, and many people in trade and industry. Thus, we must carefully examine this politically most-favored technique of dealing with imbalances in the foreign-exchange market, even if market segmentation through controls and restrictions or through explicit application of multiple exchange rates constitutes, in the eyes of an economist, a sacrifice of the "economic principle."

Discriminatory Exchange Rates

Techniques of "selective devaluation" are easily understood when they take the form of openly announced multiple exchange rates. Several developing countries have resorted to such schemes, charging lower prices for foreign currency to importers of goods regarded as more desirable, and higher prices to importers of goods regarded as less desirable, either because they are supposed to be luxury goods or because they compete with goods offered by domestic producers; and paying higher prices for foreign currency earned by exports favored for a variety of reasons, and lower prices to less favored suppliers.

Not only countries with primitive economies (and primitive economics) resort to selective devaluations or upvaluations of their currencies. Some of the richest countries have adopted such devices, though usually in forms that conceal the nature of the schemes adopted. A few examples will illustrate the point.

The United States has since 1960 taken several measures that may be characterized as concealed selective devaluations. It first devalued the military-expenditures dollar, when it ruled that the military should purchase goods and services (say, the repair of trucks) in the United States rather than overseas whenever the cost is no more than 50 per cent higher than overseas. Thus, the cost of foreign currency "saved" was anywhere up to 50 per cent above parity. The second devaluation was that of the foreign-aid dollar, when foreign aid was tied to purchases from the United States. Some aid recipients, such as the Pakistanis, found that the value of the dollars received was thereby reduced by more than 40 per cent. The third devaluation, that of the portfolio-investment dollar, was by only 15 per cent, in the form of a tax (Interest-Equalization Tax) on the purchase of foreign securities. Next came quantitative restrictions on direct investments and on bank lending abroad, which were the equivalent of devaluations of the dollars intended for such uses. The percentage of devaluation in these instances varies according to the amounts of capital exports suppressed during different periods; the more effective the restrictions the greater the equivalent reduction in the effective exchange rate of the dollar intended to be used for foreign loans and investments, that is, the reduction that would have effected the same cut in capital exports.

The United Kingdom, while still resisting an open and uniform devaluation of the pound sterling—which was eventually carried out in November 1967—resorted in 1965 to a concealed devaluation of the import-purchasing pound by imposing a 15 per cent surcharge on all imports. To devalue in this fashion the pound for importers' payments but not for exporters' receipts was to seek an improvement of the trade deficit by a reduction instead of expansion of the trade volume.

A selective upvaluation of the currency in the form of border-tax measures was carried out by Western Germany in November 1968, while the government was still resisting an open and uniform revaluation of the German mark—which was eventually carried out in the fall of 1969. This partial upvaluation, which was not really concealed, in as much as the German government spoke of

Ersatzaufwertung (substitute upvaluation), was applied to exports as well as imports, with exporters paying a tax and importers receiving a tax refund of 4 per cent.

While the rates of implicit selective devaluations are visible or calculable in cases of taxes, surcharges, tariff increases, premiums, bonuses, etc., they are matters of conjecture when direct controls or quantitative restrictions are imposed. In such cases, the analyst must first estimate the effectiveness of the measure, for example, the difference between what actually was imported and what would have been imported in the absence of the restriction; then he must estimate the difference between the domestic resale prices of the imports and the lower prices that could have been obtained for the larger quantities of unrestricted imports. Estimates are greatly facilitated if one knows the size of the bribes which importers offer to pay to the government officials who issue import licenses. The value differentials become matters of public record (or at least matters of feasible investigation) where import licenses are transferable and the prices paid for licenses are reported. This has been the practice with respect to several imports subject to licensing in India and Pakistan; the rates of concealed devaluation of their currencies were thereby known for a variety of imports.

Real and Financial Correctives

Selective measures designed to redress an imbalance of payments through differential foreign-exchange rates, through charges or bonuses, through quantitative restrictions, or through moral suasion employed to influence particular segments of the market may be called real correctives if they apply to the flow of goods and services, or financial correctives if they apply to the flow of funds, on capital account or as unilateral transfers. Among the examples given for instances of concealed devaluation we have seen several financial correctives employed by the United States.

In the case of certain measures that are supposed to be financial correctives it may be difficult to decide whether they really correct, that is, reduce or remove, an existing imbalance of payments or whether they merely finance it. The distinction between correcting and financing a deficit (or surplus) is normally made by means of operational criteria: for example, changes in monetary reserves and in "liquid" foreign claims and debts involving monetary authorities or commercial banks are treated as "monetary movements" and shown "below the line" in the statistical accounts of the balance of payments. These changes *finance* the balance of the items "above the line," whereas movements of long-term capital, movements of short-term capital not involving the banking system, and unilateral transfers are all shown above the line and may therefore correct the imbalance that would exist in their absence. This sounds easier, however, than it is in many instances: in several borderline cases the interpretation will be largely arbitrary.

The borderline cases are of three kinds:

1. Some changes in liquid liabilities to foreign banks entered as financing items (below the line) may be more appropriately regarded as financial correctives, that is, as capital inflows reducing rather than financing a deficit. This refers chiefly to those parts of the holdings of dollar balances by foreign banks with American banks that meet a sustained increase in their demand for holding cash. The probability that these balances will be firmly held, or even further increased, is much greater than the probability that they will be withdrawn tomorrow or the next day.

2. Some contrived inflows of short-term capital may be more appropriately regarded as financing items rather than as correctives. This refers to "non-liquid" funds that are more likely to flow out again than to stay. The usual operational criteria for regarding them as non-liquid (and hence placing them above the line) are the form of the credit instruments, the stated terms of maturity, and the type and nationality of debtors and creditors; the theoretical criterion, however, is the probability of quick withdrawal.

3. Some contrived changes on long-term capital account, known to be reversed before long, may be more appropriately regarded as financing items. This refers to flows of long-term capital that are almost certain to be reversed. We do not know how we could statistically divide movements of long-term capital—called long-term because of the stated terms of maturity—according to the likelihood of their reversal. But this is what really matters.

In other words, the operational definitions guiding the balance-of-payment accountants cannot do justice to the economic character of the transactions in question. Many financial correctives, producing changes in the balance of payments on capital account, will foreseeably prove of only temporary effectiveness—and will therefore merely postpone the need for real adjustment—and some will almost inevitably reverse themselves and will therefore be completely ineffective over an economically relevant period. Hence, one must frequently question the statistical or economic interpreter's decision to record as an improvement what is in fact only a device for gaining time—a financing device.

Correctives versus Adjustment

Several years ago I published an essay discussing the differences between "Real Adjustment, Compensatory Corrections, and Foreign Financing of Imbalances in International Payments."[2] I concluded that temporary financing is a stopgap, often embarrassing and, of course, of limited duration; that policies designed to bring forth the desired compensatory corrections will, more often than not, have repercussions that frustrate the attempts and, even if they work, will not be consistent with the economic principle; and that real adjustment, was therefore the only reliable cure of an imbalance in international payments.

My terminological proposals and theoretical arguments have met with severe criticism: I was rebuked for having proposed "persuasive definitions" and for having violated my own rules in concealing my value judgments by a clever choice of concepts and assumptions. I admit that some of my theoretical judgments, especially the policy implications of my arguments, may look like a sketch painted entirely in black and white, using black for what I defined as real and financial correctives, and white only for what I defined as real adjustment. I shall try elsewhere to defend my distinctions and restate my arguments in less vulnerable terms.

My arguments will be based on a number of distinctions which I consider relevant for judging the effectiveness and efficiency of measures to correct an imbalance of payments. Are the measures designed to remain in force for good or only for a time? Are they likely to have lasting or only temporary effects? Do they operate chiefly on sustainable flows or on exhaustible stocks? Do they work through market forces or rather through direct controls? Do they induce or simulate automatic processes or do they largely consist of discretionary actions? Are they universal or selective, neutral or discriminatory?

To be sure, it is not permissible to characterize corrective actions as "inefficient by definition." The probability, however, is high that research and analysis will establish that most of them are adopted as temporary makeshifts, are only temporarily effective, are discriminatory, and are inefficient. With this judgment, to be supported in another publication, I turn to the discussion of real adjustment.

How Supply and Demand Can Be Adjusted to Given Exchange Rates

There are, I repeat, in principle two ways to accomplish real adjustment: either by adjusting supply and demand to the given exchange rate or by adjusting the exchange rate to the given state of supply and demand.

The Given Exchange Rate

In explaining the first of these processes one assumes the existence of a given, uniform exchange rate. This assumption may look inconsistent with the analytical device of treating all positive and negative taxes (or quantitative restrictions) on certain types of foreign transactions as departures from uniform exchange rates. For, after all, import duties, export subsidies, quotas, and other interferences with selected international transactions exist in virtually all countries. The analyst overcomes the inconsistency by treating *existing* positive and negative taxes or restrictions on foreign transactions differently from *new* ones. The existing ones, particularly those that have been adopted for reasons other than to correct an imbalance in foreign payments, are treated as integral parts of the cost of production and of market conditions already built into the structure of costs and prices that determines supply and demand in the foreign-exchange market. The new corrective measures, however, designed to *change* supply and demand in the foreign-exchange market by changing relative costs and prices in particular segments of the economy, are treated as changes in the effective exchange rates applying to particular international transactions.

The first of the classical adjustment processes also alters supply and demand in the foreign-exchange market, but does so, not by changing the effective foreign-exchange rate for any international transactions, but instead by changing aggregate spending in the economy. An increase in aggregate spending will tend to reduce an excess supply of foreign currency; and a reduction of aggregate spending will tend to reduce an excess demand for foreign currency. Monetary and fiscal policies are the usual instruments employed to generate these processes. We shall be very classical by discussing monetary policy first, deferring the discussion of fiscal policy.

How Monetary Policy Can Help or Hinder the Demand Adjustment

Monetary policy under a system of pegged exchange rates consists of a combination of a routine practice and of current spontaneous (though frequently politically conditioned) decisions by the monetary authorities. Under a routine practice, they buy or sell foreign currency (or other foreign assets), taking the excess supply off or satisfying the excess demand in the foreign-exchange market. On the basis of spontaneous decisions (often oriented toward maintaining "desirable" interest rates), they buy or sell domestic credit instruments. If one of their objectives is to avoid a lasting imbalance in foreign payments, that is, if they want to attain "adjustment" at least eventually, if not promptly or soon, domestic credit policy must not offset all changes in their foreign-exchange holdings or in their net reserve position. Orthodox monetary policy called for much more than this: domestic credit was supposed not only to refrain from offsetting but even to reinforce the effects which the external balance was having on the stock of money and, indirectly, on the flow of aggregate spending.

Separating a routine part and a discretionary part in monetary policy may be regarded as a little unrealistic in that the discretion regarding domestic credit operations has at times, in certain countries, assumed routine character. Just as the pegging of exchange rates excludes discretion from the accumulation and disposal of foreign currency, pegging of interest rates can have the same effect upon domestic credit outstanding. Such a pegging routine can be established for loans and advances (to commercial banks or also to other types of borrowers) and for government securities bought or sold in open-market operations. For example, the central bank may accept the "duty" of maintaining the price of certain government bonds at a fixed level or within fixed limits.

Such a system, however, of pegging both interest rates and exchange rates at fixed levels could not long endure. If the central bank were to meet the demand for domestic credit at fixed interest rates, its domestic loans-and-securities portfolio would expand whenever the demand for credit increased; the resulting expansion of aggregate spending would raise the demand for foreign exchange and reduce the supply; as the central bank continued to meet the excess demand for foreign exchange at fixed exchange rates, its foreign reserves would run down and would eventually be depleted. Since the loss of the foreign reserves would terminate their ability to maintain the foreign-exchange rate, the authorities would have to choose between giving up one of the two fixed pegs, either the interest rate or the exchange rate. The greater allegiance to fixed exchange rates dictates the choice: interest rates must be allowed to vary. We may conclude, therefore, that it is correct, after all, to treat the foreign-exchange operations as routine and the domestic credit operations as discretionary.

Monetary Policy in a Surplus Country

The routine or automatic part and the discretionary part of monetary policy may pull in the same or in different directions in the aggregate-demand adjustment to restore balance in international payments. We shall describe the modus operandi first in the case of an existing surplus in the balance of payments. The routine practice of the monetary authority, buying all the foreign exchange offered, increases both its reserves of foreign assets and its liquid liabilities (notes and deposits) to holders of domestic central-bank money, especially commercial banks; the commercial banks, in turn, with both their cash reserves and their deposit liabilities to domestic holders augmented by the same amounts, find their lending capacity increased. In a system of fractional reserves, one must expect the quantity of money to rise by a multiple of the increase generated by the foreign balance, unless the central bank deliberately reduces its domestic portfolio, offsetting some or all of the increase in the foreign reserves. If the total of domestic assets (credit outstanding) of the central bank is left unchanged, the "monetary base" (stock of "high-powered money") is increased precisely by the amount of foreign exchange acquired, and the total money stock will gradually increase by some multiple of that amount. Under the orthodox rule of the gold-standard game, monetary policy would be even more expansionary in that the domestic portfolio of the central bank would also be expanded in some proportion to the increase in foreign reserves. Thus, central-bank money would increase by a multiple of the surplus in the balance of payments, and commercial-bank money would increase by a multiple of the increase in central-bank money.

This monetary expansion may be mitigated by repercussions in the capital account of the balance of payments. As the increase in the supply of domestic bank credit lowers interest rates relative to those abroad, outflows of capital (or a reduction of capital inflows) may reduce the surplus in the balance of payments. In consequence, not only the monetary expansion but also the need for real adjustment may be reduced for the time being.

Many of us may have forgotten the dimensions of multiple credit expansion that we were taught in our courses on money and banking. It is quite wholesome to recall them to our minds. Assume, just for illustrative purposes, that the central bank observes a reserve ratio of 33 1/3 per cent, and commercial banks have a reserve requirement of 10 per cent. An acquisition of $100 million worth of foreign currency may then induce the central bank to extend its domestic credit portfolio by $200 million, so that the stock of central-bank money would be increased by $300 million. If there were no paper currency and coins in circulation and all central-bank money were held by commercial banks, the banks' increased lending capacity would allow their deposit liabilities to swell by $3,000 million. With a portion of the domestic money stock held in the form of bank notes and other currency rather than deposits, the potential expansion of the total money stock would be more modest, but still rather forbidding. An explosion of a receipt of $100 million to something like $1,500 million would probably be more of an "adjustment" of the money stock than any monetary authority could countenance without alarm.

One can therefore understand why most central banks are disinclined to follow the orthodox rule calling for a credit policy that reinforces the monetary expansion generated by the external surplus balance. Indeed, most bankers will fear that even without reinforcement the multiplication of the increase in the monetary base, by way of credit expansion on the part of the commercial banks, may be too inflationary. Many central banks will therefore decide to offset at least part of the increase in their foreign-exchange holdings by a reduction of their domestic credit portfolio.

Monetary Policy in a Deficit Country

The inclination to offset the effects of routine foreign-exchange operations by means of domestic credit policy may be even greater in the case of a deficit in the balance of payments. As it sells foreign exchange from its reserves to satisfy the excess demand at fixed exchange rates, the central bank "collects" the domestic money paid by the purchasers of the foreign currency. It thereby reduces the stock of central-bank money and, in particular, the reserve balances of the commercial banks. These banks will be forced, as a result, to reduce their deposit liabilities by reducing their earning assets. Thus, if the central bank leaves the total of domestic credit outstanding unchanged, the fractional-reserve multiplier will still cause the total stock of money to decline by an amount several times the foreign-payments deficit.

The destruction of domestic money and the decline of aggregate spending would be still greater under the orthodox rules of the gold-standard game, requiring the central bank to reinforce the effects of the reduction of the foreign reserve by a reduction in its domestic portfolio. The demand deflation with consequent reduction in employment would be intolerable in most countries. Thus, the monetary authorities are unwilling to reinforce the automatic contraction resulting from the payments deficit, and usually unwilling even to let the automatic contraction take its course. They will pursue a domestic credit policy that offsets in part or in full the effects which the loss of reserve has upon the monetary base.

There are limits, of course, to the extent to which the authorities may slow down or stop the process of adjustment. As they continue to offset the automatic contractions (due to sales of foreign exchange out of reserves) by discretionary expansions of domestic credit, they perpetuate the excess demand and the decline of foreign reserves. As reserves go on declining and approach the vanishing point, the authorities must make a decision: either to give up the policy of offsetting and of avoiding the deflation of demand, incomes and employment, or to give up the fixed exchange rates. (Remember that we have ruled out the imposition of selective controls or multiple exchange rates.) Continued allegiance to fixed exchange rates dictates the decision: the credit expansion offsetting the effects of selling foreign exchange must be discontinued. There is no analogous limit to offsetting the effects of a payments surplus. For, while a continuing payments deficit may be financed only as long as foreign reserves last (except in the case of a reserve-currency country), a continuing payments surplus can be financed indefinitely through endless accumulation of foreign assets and endless creation of domestic money issued in payment for the foreign currency acquired.

In this connection I may refer to an ambitious study by Michael Michaely.[3] He examined the balance-of-payments adjustment policies of several industrial countries in order to see to what extent the monetary authorities have pursued monetary policies to help or to hinder the adjustment process. His findings, as far as they have been published, illustrate and confirm my general statements.

How the Process Is Modified in a Reserve-Currency Country

The description of the automatic contraction in the deficit country and automatic expansion in the surplus country does not fit very well the routine part of monetary policy in a country whose currency serves as international transactions currency and official reserve currency. The process in the Unites States is somewhat modified because there a payments deficit does not lead to sales of foreign exchange by the American monetary authorities and banks but rather to transfers of U.S. dollars to foreign holders, official and private. Some writers have been so impressed by this difference that they thought the adjustment mechanism could not work at all in reserve-currency countries.

Where precisely lies the essential difference and how does it modify the process? The point to start from is the fact that the Unites States *owes* the dollars which other countries *own* as official reserves or as private balances. A payments deficit for the United States shows itself in an increase in liquid liabilities to foreigners, while the payments surpluses in other countries take the form of increases in liquid dollar assets and their deficits take the form of decreases in liquid dollar assets. It is immediately evident that changes in the size of the foreign-asset portfolio of a central bank or of commercial banks change the banks' deposit liabilities, that is, the stock of a country's money, in the same direction. On the other hand, it is not immediately evident how changes in liquid dollar liabilities to foreigners are associated with the stock and velocity of U.S. money. This lack of visibility has induced some observers to assume that payments deficits have no effect upon money, liquidity, incomes, and aggregate demand in the United States. It should have been clear, however, to anybody who knows the first thing about a balance sheet that an increase in the banks' liquid liabilities to foreigners must, if nothing changes on the asset side, necessarily be associated with a decline in some other class of liabilities and that this may have important implications.

The increase in liquid liabilities to foreigners (in the form of demand deposits or time deposits and other bank debts payable in less than twelve months) may be linked with a reduction of (1) demand deposit liabilities to residents, (2) time deposit liabilities payable to residents in less than a year, (3) time deposit liabilities payable to residents in more than a year, or (4) time deposit liabilities payable to nonresidents in more than a year. The last two cases are, in all probability, instances of deficits on capital account through the outflow of American capital (in case 3) or foreign capital (in case 4) from the United States, either because of a change in differential yields or because of a change in asset preference for other reasons. We may note that ordinarily such stock adjustments are not sustainable over long periods and may therefore not call for real adjustment, that is, for changes in the flows of goods and services.

In the first two cases the reductions of bank deposits of residents probably represent reductions in active domestic circulation of money. This is almost certain when debits to demand deposits of resident individuals or corporations are the result of purchases of foreign goods, services, securities or other foreign assets. Where time deposits are held as near-money (near-cash balances), their decline may likewise involve a reduction in domestic liquidity and spending power. In these cases, payments deficits in the form of an increase in liquid liabilities to foreigners may very well result in a 1:1 reduction in the domestic money supply in the wider sense of the word. If not offset by expansions of the domestic credit portfolio of the American banks, the adjustment mechanism may be seen in operation, though not with regard to bank liquidity. In countries where deficits have to be financed through sales from official reserves, commercial banks lose balances with the central bank and may be forced—in the absence of offsetting domestic credit expansions by the central bank—to contract loans and, thereby, the stock of domestic money. This effect of the "fractional-reserve multiplier" is absent where the payments deficits are financed by mere changes in the composition of bank liabilities. Only if the foreign recipients of dollars, particularly foreign central banks, were holding them with the Federal Reserve Bank of New York would American banks lose reserves and be forced to contract their loan portfolios.

A fifth possibility has to be considered: the foreign recipients of dollars, official or private, may decide to hold them in the form of U.S. securities. In this case the outcome depends on who sells the securities in which the foreigners "invest" the dollars received. If they are sold by the Federal Reserve Bank, the adjustment process is not impeded at all; it works in high gear, including a cut in bank liquidity. If they are sold by commercial banks, the initial reduction in American domestic spending power (through the decline in resident deposits) is overcompensated by an increase in the American banks' lending power. In this case, aggregate demand in the United

States may be increased instead of reduced. Finally, if the securities are sold by American nonbank holders, aggregate demand is not affected either way and no adjustment process is initiated.

With all these possible courses of events, one cannot say with assurance to what extent an automatic adjustment process will be generated in a reserve-currency country in deficit. In any case, it is wrong to deny that the process can work; some of the roads to monetary contraction are open. Of course, that they *can* work does not mean that they will be allowed to work. Discretionary monetary policy can always prevent the contraction.

How Fiscal Policy Is Supposed to Modify the Process

In the last ten years it has been fashionable to advise governments against using monetary policy for the purpose of adjusting aggregate demand, and to recommend reliance on fiscal policy instead. Such advice has been considered particularly pertinent for the treatment of "dilemma cases." These are cases in which the attainment of domestic goals and of external balance would call for opposite changes in effective demand. There have been countries that suffered from payments deficits and underemployment at the same time; they would need monetary contraction to reduce the external deficit but expansion to reduce unemployment. Other countries have been suffering from payments surpluses and price inflation simultaneously; they would need monetary expansion to reduce the surplus but contraction to reduce price increases. The single instrument of domestic monetary policy would clearly be inappropriate for attaining or approaching both targets; to improve one disorder would be to worsen the other.

The use of a second policy instrument was indicated: Fiscal policy was assigned to deal with the domestic disorders—unemployment or price inflation—while monetary policy was to deal with the external imbalance—the deficit or surplus in foreign payments at fixed exchange rates. How were the two instruments supposed to modify the adjustment process? The idea was that monetary policy should not be used to affect aggregate demand but rather to establish such differentials in interest rates as would induce international flows of capital that could correct the imbalance in foreign payments. In other words, aggregate demand was to be changed by fiscal policy in order to create more employment or to stop price inflation, while the imbalance of payments was not to be treated by real adjustment, that is, by an adjustment of the flow of goods and services. Instead, capital movements induced by interest-rate differentials should establish external balance and thus remove the need for real adjustment.

I have serious doubts in the long-run effectiveness of such policies. I presented the arguments explaining this skepticism in my essay, "In Search of Guides for Policy."[4] I shall not repeat them here. What should be discussed here, however, is the question whether fiscal policy can extend the limits to which offsetting policy can be employed to slow down or stop the process of demand adjustment under fixed exchange rates.

The policy mix prescribed in cases of payments surplus combined with price inflation is to create a budget surplus (to tax more, spend less, reduce government debt) in order to reduce aggregate demand, and to use monetary ease and lower domestic interest rates in order to drive out and repel capital. The prescription of lower interest rates implies expansionary monetary policy and militates, therefore, against the use of offsetting the automatic expansion (which goes with the payments surplus) by the use of deliberate contraction of domestic credit.

The policy mix prescribed in cases of payments deficit combined with underemployment is fiscal ease (tax less, spend more, borrow more) in order to increase domestic spending, and monetary restraint in order to raise interest rates and attract capital from abroad and keep it from going abroad. Monetary restraint is clearly incompatible with an expansionary credit policy designed to offset the automatic contraction that goes with the payments deficit.

We conclude therefore that in dilemma cases the use of fiscal policy to relieve monetary policy from its function of adjusting aggregate demand does not widen the scope of offsetting. (One might reach this conclusion by inferring it from the exclusive assignment of monetary policy to deal with external balance or imbalances.)

This conclusion does not hold for non-dilemma cases, when the same monetary policy could improve both domestic and external disorders.

In the case of a payments deficit associated with price inflation, monetary restraint is indicated as remedial policy for both. By simultaneous fiscal restraint—higher taxes, lower expenditures, debt reduction—the fiscal authorities can probably relieve the burden of the monetary authorities. There is some inconsistency, however, in the effect upon interest rates. Reductions in the public debt tend to lower interest rates while monetary restraint is supposed to raise interest rates enough to attract capital from abroad and keep capital from going abroad. Still, if the fiscal restraint succeeds in inactivating some cash balances (reducing the velocity of circulation) it may be possible to relax the degree of monetary contraction and thus go a little farther in offsetting some of the automatic contraction genera·ed by the payments deficit.

In the case of a payments surplus associated with underemployment, monetary expansion is indicated as remedial policy for both. By simultaneous fiscal ease—lower taxes, higher expenditures, governmental borrowing—the fiscal authorities can perhaps assist the monetary authorities, and thus allow them to offset through credit restraint a larger part of the expansion generated by the payments surplus. But since fiscal ease and monetary ease have opposite effects upon interest rates, the effectiveness of the policy mix is, as in the previous case, less than certain. The theory of the policy mix relies heavily on interest-rate effects: in the present case, lower interest rates are supposed to repel and expel capital funds, and higher interest rates are supposed to increase the velocity of circulation, but interest rates cannot be lower and higher at the same time.

Some practical policy mixers think probably less of interest-rate effects and more of time lags; they expect fiscal policy to aid monetary policy less through effects upon velocity and more through effects upon the demand for bank credit; they expect fiscal policy to have a more immediate effect upon aggregate spending than changes in the lending capacity of commercial banks may have. Whether these expectations are justified depends largely on whether the fiscal measures operate through government expenditures or through changes in taxation.

A Digression: The Theory of the Policy Mix

Although it is not an essential part of my assignment, it may be a desirable digression to make a few explanatory statements about the definitions of monetary and fiscal policy. The most acceptable definitions have monetary policy control the quantity of money, and fiscal policy control the government's tax revenues, expenditures, and debts. The controversy between the monetarists and the fiscalists centers on the question whether changes in aggregate spending (or effective demand) are better accomplished and better explained by changes in the money stock or by changes in the government's budget. The difference becomes sharp only if the fiscalist position is stated as asserting significant effects of fiscal policy upon effective demand without any changes in the money *stock*. This would confine its effects upon aggregate spending to activation or inactivation of existing money balances.

In actual practice one finds fiscal and monetary policy so closely interrelated that one can easily understand why economists may differ in their emphasis on the one or the other. Monetary policy, through its effects upon aggregate income, will affect the government's budget, changing both tax revenues and expenditures; and fiscal policy, through its effects on the credit market, will affect the lending activities of the banks and thus the quantity of money. It would take a special effort for the fiscal authorities to keep the budget unchanged while the money stock is changed; and it would be similarly difficult for the monetary authorities to keep the stock of money unchanged while taxes, expenditures, and debts of the government are changed. Only in theory, not in practice, can monetary and fiscal policy be cleanly separated.

There is an interesting analogy between the effects of expansionary fiscal policy ("fiscal ease") and the phenomenon of wage-push inflation. A wage push is inflationary only if it is supported by monetary expansion; without it, it leads to increasing unemployment. A policy of fiscal ease, likewise, is strongly expansionary only if lax monetary controls permit an increase in the supply of bank loans and money; without it, it leads to higher interest rates and reduced expenditures by would-be borrowers, who are "outbid" and thus frustrated in their plans to invest or in their propensities to consume. (In both cases, this statement refers to sustained expansions, not just little spurts.) A wage push is usually accompanied by an increase in the demand for loans, by business for larger working capital, by consumers for purchases of durable goods, and by government for the finance of expenditures to maintain income and employment. Fiscal ease is usually accompanied by an increase in the demand for loans, by the government for the finance of its increase in expenditures or reduction in taxes, by business for increased investments, and by consumers for purchases of durables. In both cases, therefore, monetary policy is brought into the picture: the monetary authorities have to decide whether they should allow the banking system to meet some of the increased demand for credit and thereby to increase the stock of money.

Returning to the question how fiscal and monetary policies can be distinguished, I propose that we find the characteristic effects of fiscal policy in the associated increase or reduction of the *demand* for credit and *demand* for money, whereas we see the characteristic role of monetary policy in the control of the *supply* of bank credit and thereby the *supply* of money.

How Aggregate Demand Can Adjust Supply and Demand for Foreign Exchange

We can at last move on to answer the question how changes in aggregate demand cause the supply and demand functions in the foreign-exchange market to shift. We shall keep in mind that the shifts implied in "real adjustment" are those of the supply of foreign currency by exporters and the demand for foreign currency by importers of goods and services.

We begin again with the case of a surplus in the balance of payments and the classical reaction through an expansionary monetary policy, leading to an increase in aggregate demand, incomes, liquidity, investment, consumption, and prices. As a result, the demand for imports will increase, partly because of larger investment, partly because of higher incomes, and partly because of higher prices of domestic products and services. In addition, the supply of exports will decline, as their producers find easier outlets in domestic markets and, moreover, may find that higher production costs make it harder for them to accept the prices they can get in foreign markets. The increase in the demand for imports brings with it an increase in the demand for foreign exchange to pay for the imports; and the reduction in the supply of exports ordinarily brings with it a reduction in the supply of foreign exchange received for exports.

If we visualize the curves depicting supply and demand in the foreign-exchange market, the initial surplus in the balance of payments is represented by an excess supply of foreign currency at the fixed price for foreign currency. That is to say, the two curves intersect at a point below the pegged price, forcing the monetary authorities to take the excess supply off the market. The adjustment generated by the increase in aggregate spending is now shown by shifts of the two curves: the demand curve moves upward and to the right, the supply curve upward and to the left. The intersection of the two curves is thereby moved higher, so that the excess supply is gradually reduced, until it becomes zero when the intersection (the equilibrium price in this market) is lifted to the fixed level. (Needless to say, price inflation is an integral part of this process.)

Now to the case of a deficit in foreign payments. The classical reaction is a contractionary monetary policy. When most countries grow, and a certain degree of monetary expansion is warranted to permit growth without inflation, the monetary policy appropriate to restoring balance in foreign payments need not be absolutely contractionary; *relative* contraction, that is, expansion at distinctly slower rates than those abroad, especially those in surplus countries, may suffice. Such a policy of merely relative contraction prolongs, of course, the period of adjustment, sometimes for years. The process is more easily understood if it is first analysed as involving *absolute* contraction of aggregate spending.

The contraction will be associated with reductions in effective demand, incomes, liquidity, investment, consumption, and employment. As a result, the demand for imports will decline, partly because of smaller investment, partly because of lower incomes (chiefly due to fewer hours of work and reduced employment), and partly because prices of domestic products and services may become lower relative to those of imported products. In addition, the supply of exports will increase, as their producers, faced with a shrinkage of domestic markets, are forced to look for outlets in foreign markets and, moreover, may now find prices abroad relatively more attractive. The reduction of the demand for imports brings with it a reduction in the demand for foreign exchange to pay for imports; and the increase in the supply of exports ordinarily brings with it an increase in the supply of foreign exchange received from exports.

Translating all this into the customary graphic representation, we visualize the initial situation of deficit in the balance of payments as an excess demand for foreign currency at its fixed price. That is to say, the curves depicting supply and demand in the foreign-exchange market intersect at a point above the pegged price for foreign currency, forcing the monetary authorities to satisfy the excess demand by sales from their exchange reserves. The adjustment generated by the reduction in aggregate spending is shown by shifts of the two curves: the demand curve for foreign currency moves downward and to the left, the supply curve downward and to the right. The intersection of the two curves is thereby moved down, so that the excess demand is gradually reduced, until it becomes zero when the intersection is lowered to the fixed level. (It will be understood that unemployment is likely to play a major role in this process.)

We should mark here a significant asymmetry between the process that removes a surplus and the process that removes a deficit in the balance of payments: the contraction of effective demand in deficit countries causes a reduction in *employment*, while the expansion of effective demand in surplus countries causes an increase in *prices*. This asymmetry is conditioned by institutional factors; they account for asymmetrical reactions in the labor market.

HOW THE EXCHANGE RATE CAN BE ADJUSTED TO SUPPLY AND DEMAND

Now that we have explored the processes by which supply and demand can be adjusted to a given exchange rate, we reverse the question and ask how the exchange rate can be adjusted to given conditions of supply and demand. We must understand, of course, that conditions rarely stay "given" for any length of time; they change under the impact of all sorts of measures or events. But "approximately given" is sufficient for our purposes when we refer to supply and demand, and "approximately adjusted," when we refer to the exchange rate. Only freely flexible exchange rates can be regarded as perfectly adjusted in that they move to the level at which the amounts of foreign currency supplied and demanded on any particular day are equal.

Automatic and Discretionary Adjustments

In our discussion of monetary policy we distinguished a routine or automatic part and a discretionary part. A parallel distinction is applicable to exchange-rate policy. Full flexibility, freely floating rates, would make the price movements of foreign currency completely automatic; and under a system of limited flexibility—for example, within a wider band around a given parity—the movements would be automatic in so far as the monetary authorities refrained from intervening in the foreign-exchange market. On the other hand, decisions by the authorities to intervene through sales or purchases at rates that are not absolutely fixed constitute the discretionary part of exchange-rate policy. Changes in official par values are always discretionary. Some economists have tried to reduce the scope of discretion and develop formulas for the guidance of parity adjusters; but these efforts have been entirely academic and will probably remain academic for years to come.

An old terminological convention, though violated by many writers, reserves the use of "depreciation" and "appreciation" for automatic variations of exchange rates, and "devaluation" and "revaluation" (or, more clearly, "upvaluation") for discretionary changes of par values. The former changes are the results of free-market forces, as competing would-be sellers pull the price of foreign currency down when they cannot find ready outlets, and competing would-be buyers pull the price up when they cannot find the amounts of currency they are seeking. Parity changes, on the other hand, are the result of judgment (or of compromise between conflicting judgments) and such judgments may be far off the mark. A parity adjustment in a single stroke can at best be roughly correct, but will more likely be excessive or inadequate. As was said earlier, parity adjusters usually do not even attempt to hit the "equilibrium rate"; if they adjust the parity of an overvalued currency, they prefer to devalue so much that they can start replenishing their depleted exchange reserves; and if they adjust the parity of an undervalued currency, they may prefer to raise it by less than the amount that would immediately stop the payments surplus, because they expect that the demand expansion generated by the reserve accumulation may not yet have run its full course.

Exchange-Rate Adjustment and Money Supply

An operational difference between depreciation (or appreciation), on the one hand, and devaluation (or upvaluation), on the other, lies in the participation of the monetary authorities in the foreign-exchange market. If they allow the currency to depreciate (or appreciate) in the market, the authorities refrain from intervening through sales or purchases. But if they devalue (or upvalue) the currency, they declare their intention to sell or buy at pegged rates. Consequently, the effects of depreciation (or appreciation) of the currency in the foreign-exchange market differ from those of devaluation (or upvaluation) with regard to the supply of central-bank money. Depreciation (or appreciation) does not affect that supply; devaluation (or upvaluation), however, creates or cancels central-bank money in the process of official sales or purchases of foreign exchange. These differences have implications regarding the "given" conditions of supply and demand in that the changes in the stock of money that are associated with devaluation (or upvaluation) are likely to alter these conditions.

It follows that an analysis of the effects of devaluation or upvaluation cannot be complete without explicit stipulations concerning monetary policy in both its routine and its discretionary operations. Only in a first approximation may one speak of the effects of exchange-rate adjustments upon foreign trade without stating what happens to the amount of money and aggregate spending.

In the absence of direct controls and quantitative restrictions, an increase in the external exchange value of a currency (that is, a reduction in the price of foreign currency) will reduce a payments surplus (that is, an excess supply of foreign exchange); and, conversely, a reduction in the external exchange value of a currency (that is, an increase in the price of foreign currency) will reduce a payments deficit (that is, an excess demand for foreign exchange). These statements, questioned in some quarters 15 or 20 years ago, can now, after much research and analysis, be made with almost apodictic assuredness. Some economists, in endorsing these statements, rely on the contributions which capital movements can make to restoring balance when disaligned exchange rates are realigned. These corrective capital movements, however, may be interpreted as merely temporary finance of the imbalance and as actual retardation of the real-adjustment process. Such retardation, though it may be desirable, should not be regarded as an essential part of the process. The essence of the process is the effect on the international flows of goods and services.

Degrees of Adjustment of the Supply of Exports

The effects on these real flows can be analyzed in various phases or stages: (1) before any *prices* of goods and services are affected in terms of the domestic moneys of the countries where they are produced; (2) after the changes in quantities demanded due to the change in exchange rates have affected the *supply prices* of the goods and services in domestic moneys of the producing countries; (3) after the changes in these prices have affected the *quantities produced* of these goods and services with given productive facilities; and (4) after the production of these goods and services have been further affected by *adaptations in the productive facilities*. Technical economic parlance uses such expressions as instantaneous impact, short run, medium run, and long run to distinguish among these phases or stages, and some analysts make even finer distinctions. It may be appropriate, in addition, to consider time lags of deliveries behind contracts. However, to take account of all these lags, transitions, and adaptation periods but still to disregard changes in the money supply, occurring partly as a result of the induced changes in foreign trade, is one of those analytical procedures that one cannot help finding excessively unrealistic—unless he knows that analysis, in the literal sense of the word, breaks things apart which in reality are inseparably fused together.

How It All Works

This, then, is how exchange-rate adjustment works in the case of an initial surplus of the balance of payments: The reduced price of foreign currency reduces the cost of imported products in domestic currency; this will cause an increase in the quantity of imports demanded, as spending power is switched partly from domestic products and partly from domestic liquidity (through reduced demand for cash balances and increased willingness to incur debt). The reduced price of foreign currency also reduces the receipts of exporters in domestic currency*; this will cause the quantity of exports supplied to decrease, as output is switched from foreign to domestic markets, with the incidental result that consumers are induced by the availability of "better buys" to reduce their liquidity.

In the case of an initial deficit in the payments balance the sequence works as follows: The increased price of foreign currency raises the cost of imported products in domestic currency; this will cause the quantity of imports demanded to decline, as spending power is switched from imports partly to domestic products and partly to increased liquidity (through increased demand for cash balances and reduced willingness to incur debt). The increased price of foreign currency also increases the receipts of exporters in domestic currency; this will cause the quantity of exports supplied to increase, as output is switched from domestic to foreign markets, with the incidental result that consumers, squeezed out of the market by increased prices, may be induced to hold more liquid funds.

Money Matters

I have stressed the effects of exchange-rate adjustments upon domestic liquidity along with the switches of expenditures between

---

*Whether exports are invoiced in domestic or in foreign money makes no difference for new business; if contract prices are stated in foreign money, their equivalent in domestic money is reduced; if they are stated in domestic money, these prices will have to be lower for given quantities to be salable abroad.

domestic and foreign markets. The reason is that the effects on trade will be lasting only if they are accompanied by induced changes in the demand for money balances—and if these changes are not completely offset by monetary policy. If the monetary authorities make the mistake of matching the induced changes in the demand for money with equal (or even larger) changes in the supply of money, the redress of the imbalance of payments will be only temporary.

Several countries have learned these facts of life only by experience and to their great chagrin. The theory is not, however, so very difficult to grasp. In the case of a payments deficit, currency devaluation is supposed to reduce the real spending power of the people who have been overspending. For the effects of devaluation to be sustained, it is essential *not* to replace the loss of buying power by expansions of the money stock. If the supply of money is gradually increased—beyond the normal rate of real growth—the effects of the devaluation will be dissipated, sometimes even more quickly than the positive effects upon the trade balance can materialize.

The fact that monetary restraint is required if the effects of devaluation upon the trade balance are to materialize and to last has inspired some skeptics to ask why devaluation was indicated at all, since monetary restraint alone, without exchange-rate adjustment, could do the job of restoring balance. The question is naive. A deflation sufficient to remove a large and persistent deficit at an unchanged exchange rate is something totally different from the mere avoidance of money inflation (or reflation) required for the success of a devaluation. The demand deflation at an unchanged exchange rate would call for a destruction of money that takes away enough of the people's cash balances to force them to stop overspending; "dehydrating" the economy to this extent would surely produce large unemployment. The monetary restraint required to supplement devaluation need not do anything of the sort; it must only avoid restoring the purchasing power of the people which the higher prices of imports and of exportables have absorbed in consequence of the higher price of foreign currency.

MUTUALLY EXCLUSIVE ALTERNATIVES
OR COMPLEMENTS?

The prescription to use some degree of monetary restraint in combination with devaluation may have suggested to the reader that the two approaches to real adjustment are not mutually exclusive but can be used in combination. Our early formulations may have given the impression of an either-or relationship: as if monetary authorities had to opt either for inflation-deflation or for upvaluation-devaluation as the principal routes to external balance. This impression, however, would be wrong. A payments surplus can be removed by a combination of demand inflation with upvaluation, and a payments deficit by a combination of demand deflation with devaluation. Where the authorities prefer to use floating exchange rates, for a transition period or as a permanent system, the words upvaluation and devaluation in the preceding sentence have to be replaced by appreciation and depreciation of the currency. In any case, aggregate-demand adjustment and exchange-rate adjustment are not mutually exclusive, but cooperant approaches to the real-flow adjustment required to restore balance in foreign payments.

Combining the Two Strategies

Thus, a country with a persistent surplus in the balance of payments may decide to have a part of it whittled away by demand-and-price inflation and to remove the other part by an upvaluation of its currency (or by an appreciation under floating rates). This may be a conscious decision by its monetary authorities based on a judgment that they ought not to impose on the economy too large a rate of inflation, which they would find socially and economically harmful because of the distorting effects while it was going on and which they could later stop or slow down only at a substantial social and economic cost.

Likewise, a country with a persistent deficit in the balance of payments may decide to have a part of it removed by a demand-and-employment deflation, and the rest, probably the larger part, by devaluation (or by depreciation under floating rates). To do all of it by deflation would appear to most governments as too costly and painful.

The combined use of aggregate-demand adjustment and exchange-rate adjustment to bring about the real-flow adjustment required for balance is more likely to be adopted in surplus countries than in deficit countries. Surplus countries usually do not mind a dose of price inflation in a world in which inflation has become endemic. Deficit countries, however, are less inclined to use both demand deflation and devaluation; after all, they resort to devaluation in order to avoid deflation with severe unemployment and, if they overcome all the political obstacles that make the decision to devalue so hard, they will not accept unemployment on top of it. Since the authorities will have pleaded that devaluation is necessary in order to avoid the high rate of unemployment that would be associated with demand deflation, they will try to devalue sufficiently, if not excessively, in order to maintain employment at a high level or to bring it to an even higher level.

Interprovincial Adjustment with Demand Effects Only

The adjustment process restoring interprovincial balance within a country cannot use exchange-rate changes, but must rely on demand effects only. This raises the question why, if the process can work within an area with a uniform currency, alterations of exchange rates should be required or desired for adjustment between areas with different currencies. What is so different between interprovincial and international imbalances of payments and the adjustment process restoring balance?

Disequilibrating Forces

From the catalogue of disequilibrating or disaligning forces, most of them apply to different provinces as well as to different countries. A few, however, do not. There cannot be substantial changes in differential taxation and in interprovincial trade restrictions; and, most importantly, there cannot be large differences in the growth of the supply of money. The latter differences, though, cannot be completely excluded, since the initial spending of newly created money may be concentrated in particular provinces, say, where large investments by private industry or by public agencies are undertaken. But the spilling-over of new money stocks into other provinces need not cause any balance-of-payments difficulties, since the same central bank and probably the same commercial banks owe the liabilities that serve as money throughout the country.

Other disequilibrating forces can cause imbalances in interprovincial payments. There can be differential rates of growth of the labor force, of capital investment, of productivity, of total real product; there can be differential changes in wage rates and in prices of products produced only in particular provinces; there can be provincial differences in propensities to spend and to save; there can be changes in supply and demand of goods and services and, of course, there can be changes in capital movements from province to province.

Why Demand Adjustment Works Better

Absence of information about such imbalances and their adjustment is probably the biggest difference between interprovincial and international trade, and finance. However, not only politico-psychological, but also some other factors alleviate the pains of the demand adjustments working to remove interprovincial imbalance. Demand deflation may cause serious unemployment in the deficit provinces, but the mobility of labor within a country is usually greater than across national borders, so that the unemployed may move to jobs in the surplus provinces. Moreover, fiscal aid between provinces is built into national systems of taxation and expenditures by the national government.

Whether offsetting credit policies are more likely to alleviate provincial deflation than they are to alleviate national deflation is not clear. If the demand for credit in the deficit provinces becomes more urgent than in the surplus provinces, it is conceivable that a reallocation of the national credit supply partially restores the spending power that the deficit provinces have lost. On the other hand, if the banks' business is nationwide, rather than concentrated in particular provinces, it is more plausible to assume that they would rather increase their loans to clients in the expanding surplus provinces than to those in the provinces where business is declining owing to the deflation of demand.

No information is available to decide this question. I am inclined to believe that the interprovincial adjustment process works with reasonable effectiveness because aggregate-demand adjustment is allowed to function, depressing the deficit provinces and stimulating the surplus provinces. If the individual provinces had their own central banks, charged with the duty of maintaining high levels of employment and high rates of provincial growth, we would no doubt find that offsetting credit expansions in the deficit provinces would retard demand adjustment, and interprovincial imbalances of payments would become chronic.

Optimal Currency Areas

The fact that parts of a single-currency area have only one adjustment mechanism at their disposal, since exchange-rate adjustment is ruled out, does not mean that some of these parts (provinces, areas, countries) would not be better off with separate currencies and with the possibility of exchange-rate adjustment. What is optimal for an area as a whole need not be optimal for each of its parts separately. It stands to reason that the combined welfare of all the people in the area is better served by a single currency for all. This does not, however, imply that the welfare of the people in some part of the area might not be greater if they had monetary autonomy and could achieve real-flow adjustment by adjustments of exchange rates rather than aggregate demand.

I have mentioned this not in order to give aid and comfort to separatist movements; on the contrary, I believe that in the long run most small countries would gain by joining a larger currency area, even if this meant that aggregate-demand adjustment became the sole mechanism of maintaining and restoring balance in international payments. But the "simulation" of a large currency area by maintaining fixed exchange rates among countries with separate currencies and autonomous central banks is a completely different thing. If a country defends its monetary sovereignty, it evidently wishes to put its separate welfare above the combined welfare of a group of countries to which it belongs. And if it uses its sovereignty to pursue monetary policies intended to serve its own national objectives, it would be inconsistent to submit to costly deflations and inflations of demand and prices which could be avoided by adjustments of foreign-exchange rates.

THE COST OF ADJUSTMENT

The preceding analysis of the alternative adjustment processes has probably conveyed a suggestion that the social and economic cost is heavier in the case of aggregate-demand adjustment than in the case of exchange-rate adjustment. Such a judgment, however, can be confirmed only by more considered argument, preceded by a clarification of what kind of costs may be involved.

Economic and Social Costs

Every economic change whatsoever hurts some and benefits others. Whether there is a net benefit or a net cost to the nation or community as a whole is a question that can be answered only by means of welfare analysis, unless one is satisfied with a few primitive rules of thumb. This we shall be. Total real output measured by market prices, but deflated by general price changes, will be taken as a rough index of economic welfare, though uncompensated changes in income distribution will be taken account of in memorandum fashion. If social cost is sometimes mentioned separately from economic cost, the implication is that some nonmeasurable hardship is incurred in addition to the measurable economic cost.

A special feature of real adjustment is that the changes in the flows of goods and services which restore external balance imply *intertemporal* comparisons. As a surplus in the balance of payments is reduced or removed by a reduction in the export surplus (or increase in the import surplus) the nation increases its home investment or its current consumption or both, and reduces its accumulation of foreign liquid assets; thus current "real intake" is increased, possibly at the expense of potential future intake, though the productivity of additional home investments may be so much larger than the yield of liquid foreign reserves that future intake need not suffer from a smaller build-up of foreign reserves. Obversely, as a deficit in the balance of payments is reduced or removed by an increase in the export surplus (or reduction in the import surplus) the nation reduces its home investment or its current consumption or both, and increases its foreign reserves or reduces its liquid foreign debts; thus present real intake is reduced for the sake of greater import-buying power in the future.

Intertemporal switches of this sort make it particularly difficult to judge whether they involve economic gains or losses for the nation. If an individual decides to forego consumption and capital improvements so that he can get into a more liquid position—holding more cash—one usually assumes that he knows what he is doing and that he does it because he considers it the best thing to do. However, if a central bank accumulates foreign reserves which the nation's producers have received as proceeds for an export surplus—a surplus that is the result of monetary, fiscal, wage, and exchange-rate policies—one cannot assume that the piling-up of reserves represents a conscious decision to forego national consumption and domestic investment for the sake of additional liquidity. Those who decide on the policies in question are not the same people that have to sacrifice consumption or investment, and the authorities do not even try to evaluate these sacrifices to compare them with any future gains which the nation may derive from the additional liquidity acquired. The economist may have to make a cost-benefit analysis on the basis of his own judgment of the people's attitudes. Often, however, he can identify the actual preferences of the governments as they reveal their objectives through some of their measures, particularly if the manifest intent of these measures is consistent with official declarations. In these instances the benefits and costs of real-flow adjustment can be sized up more objectively.

The "Burden" of Adjustment

Some economists have spoken of the "burden" of adjustment, but left it to their audience to figure out whether they meant "responsibility" for taking action initiating adjustment, or "hardships and losses" associated with the process of adjustment, or the "cost" of the measures used to induce the process. The notion of hardships and losses associated with the process is again ambiguous. In the case of a country reducing or removing a deficit in its foreign payments by increasing exports and reducing imports, there will be the following hardships and losses: (1) the reduction in current domestic consumption and investment as resources are switched from home use to foreign use, (2) the possible decline in productivity if the efficiency of productive factors is lower in the new uses, (3) the possible losses of income if labor previously employed in the production for the home market is immobile and becomes unemployed, and (4) the possible losses of capital if fixed equipment is specific to the old uses and becomes abundant, and therefore worthless. The first "loss" is inevitable; it is implied in the termination of the deficit; it is not the consequence and not the precondition of adjustment: It *is* the adjustment. The other three losses are incidental to the process of adjustment; they need not occur, and will not occur if labor and capital can be easily transferred without loss of productivity. Indeed, it is conceivable that productivity is increased in the new employment of the productive factors. On the other hand, the losses may be large, especially if industry is not diversified but confined to a small number of products.

These four burdens, hardships, or losses must again be distinguished from the costs of the methods used to induce the process of adjustment. Adjustment consists of the transfer of resources, but this transfer can be initiated and promoted by alternative techniques. Assume, for example, that real flows have to be altered so as to increase exports and reduce imports. Higher prices obtained for goods exported or lower costs of producing these goods would both stimulate exports, as would the mere decline in domestic demand. Lower incomes would reduce imports, but higher prices of imported goods would do it too. Changes in demand, changes in cost, changes in prices may have the same effects on sales but different effects on profits. If labor has to move to other jobs, workers may be induced to make the same change either when they lose the job they have had or when the new job offers more pay than the old. The effect, the reallocation of labor, may be the same, but in one case it is brought about by the misery of unemployment, in the other case by the attraction of better wages. It should thus be clear that different techniques chosen to initiate and promote the process of adjustment may have different economic and social costs.

The Alternative Techniques

If the distinctions between the various burdens, hardships, losses, and costs associated with the adjustment process, its initiation, and its completion are understood, many contentions will be recognized as silly misconceptions.

Take, for a change, the case of a payments surplus and the adjustment required to restore balance. Adjustment consists in a reduction of exports or an increase in imports or both. With full employment and full utilization of capacity, labor and other productive resources have to be moved from industries producing for export, and from industries producing goods competing with imports, to industries producing for the home market producer goods and/or consumer goods or services that have not been imported. The decline in the export industries and in the import-competing industries in this case is neither a burden nor a cost to the economy. On the contrary, this decline is an integral part of the transfer of resources that allows the nation to increase its current consumption and its home investment. If the reallocation can be accomplished without reduction of productivity, with only frictional unemployment, and with modest losses of capital, the present net gain to the economy may be substantial. But the alternative techniques of engineering the transfer of resources will have different costs. The classical technique of expanding aggregate demand will work through raising the prices of final and intermediate goods, raising the wages of labor, and raising the cost of production. The cost increase will be largely the result of the increased demand for labor and materials on the part of industries for whose products the increased domestic incomes are spent; it will reduce the profits of all other industries, in particular, the export industries. The export industries will be forced, through cost increases, to give up the resources now demanded for home use. With exchange-rate adjustment, the same effect is created by a reduction in the exporters' sales proceeds as the reduced price of foreign currency lowers the producers' receipts in domestic money.

Two fundamental mistakes, especially widespread among spokesmen for the export industry, in countries in heavy payments surplus, are (1) that the decline in exports is represented as an economic loss (instead of a present gain to the economy) and (2) that the (immediate) decline in profits due to a reduced price of foreign currency is foreseen but the (less immediate) decline in profits due to increased production cost in the course of the demand inflation is not foreseen. If adjustment is to be complete, the same amount of resources has to be given up by the export industry and, hence, it is quite short-sighted to point to the one force but disregard the other. There is perhaps a saving grace that gives this second mistake a measure of justification: Exchange-rate adjustment has some of its effects without delay, while aggregate-demand adjustment works gradually. If the economy keeps growing, the bite of demand inflation will be mitigated by the continuous increase in the labor force, which may allow a relative reallocation of the nation's resources and thus a merely relative decline of the export industry instead of an absolute one. If it is mainly because of this time factor that the export industrialists prefer demand inflation over currency upvaluation, one may suggest that exchange-rate adjustment need not be so abrupt either; with gliding or gradual adjustments of exchange rates the bite of price changes can be just as gradual as the gradual adjustments of aggregate demand.

The Possibility of Reversal

The last-mentioned argument in favor of gradual and against prompt and radical adjustment can also be supported by another consideration: the possibility of a reversal of the payments trend. Although most governments and monetary authorities can reasonably be charged with an almost childish optimism, which causes them to defer remedial action in the hope that the imbalance will soon disappear without any drastic measures, one cannot deny that they have been right in some instances. History records cases where things turned around and the resistance of governments to actions recommended by economic consultants was vindicated. When a large and presumably persistent deficit or surplus disappeared without adjustments of the exchange rate and without drastic adjustment of aggregate demand, one could rightly praise the patience of the authorities in refusing to submit to a "bloody operation" and in waiting for recovery without surgery. Mild medication in the form of a little monetary restraint or of a bit of monetary ease was then, apparently, the wiser solution. That an *unnecessary* devaluation or upvaluation of the currency is a social and economic cost and waste cannot be questioned.

It is illegitimate, however, to compare mild and gradual monetary medication with radical exchange-rate surgery. It is true that past experience and institutions have excluded mild and gradual exchange-rate adjustments, so that most men in charge of monetary affairs cannot think of variations in exchange rates as anything but abrupt, one-time actions by government. This need not be so. Adjustments of exchange rates can be made just as mild, gradual, and reversible as the adjustments of bank rates, open-market operations, reserve requirements, and credit ceilings have been. Devaluations need not always be by 10, or 15 per cent or more; only if they have been delayed unduly long will it be meaningless to make them much smaller. Just as bank rates can be raised or lowered by one-half of a per cent at a time and just as nobody expects them to stay unchanged for long, exchange rates can be given a degree of flexibility that dispels the notion that any change is a drastic, irreversible, one-time action. In a system of greater flexibility of exchange rates, the argument regarding the social and economic cost of unnecessary devaluations and revaluations becomes irrelevant.

The Differential Costs

We are now ready to state our conclusions. Our evaluation of the differential costs of techniques of removing or reducing an existing imbalance in foreign payments may include, besides the two methods of initiating and promoting real adjustment, the category of devices discussed under the heading of selective real correctives.

Selective correctives can be justified at best as a makeshift for a few months. Their effectiveness is so doubtful in the long run and their efficiency so low that, from an economic point of view, they are not serious substitutes for real adjustment. In actual fact, they are the most widely used measures to deal with imbalances of foreign payments, first, because most men in government lack the economic understanding required for an appraisal of the measures, and second, because special-interest groups can be served extraordinarily well by discriminatory devices. To attempt changing the international flow of goods and services by means of selective actions, restricting or promoting particular kinds of exports or imports, is to choose the most costly of all possible techniques.

Adjustment of real flows by means of adjustment of aggregate demand can be justified only where the same demand adjustment serves domestic balance. If cost-and-price inflation is to be combated by monetary and fiscal restraint, or if unemployment is to be relieved by monetary and fiscal ease, a government may well decide to impose upon the nation the effects of contracting or expanding aggregate demand. However, to choose these techniques for the sole purpose of restoring balance in foreign payments is to inflict unnecessary costs and hardships upon the people. It is an avoidable waste to induce a transfer of resources by reducing or increasing aggregate spending.

Adjustment of real flows by means of adjustment of exchange rates is the least-cost option. The price mechanism works much more cheaply than the stop-go techniques of monetary demand regulation. Changes in relative prices with stable total demand can steer the productive resources of the nation into the uses required by the situation without the wastes, disruptions, and distortions associated with flooding the economy with additional money or dehydrating it in deflationary action. Large groups of people can be badly harmed by aggregate-demand adjustment: those who have saved and hold debt-assets are hurt by price inflation, as are all those whose money incomes do not rise with the price level; and those who lose their jobs as a result of demand deflation suffer even worse hardships. But apart from the hardship inflicted upon the victimized groups, the economy loses real output in the course of inflationary and deflationary developments. Price inflation results in total production being distorted—"wrong" products being produced*—and deflation with the consequent unemployment results in total production being reduced below its potential. One must of course not assume that the reallocation of resources engineered by exchange-rate and relative-price adjustments will be without friction and without loss. But any such friction and loss will be suffered regardless of the technique chosen. The costs of demand adjustment—price inflation or unemployment—are additional to the costs of the resources switch.

A SIMPLE EPILOGUE

Adjustment hurts, and fast adjustment hurts especially badly. Adjustment from a surplus position calls for a reduction in exports, painful to export producers, who see their costs go up and their foreign markets shrink and some of these markets altogether lost; and it calls for an increase in imports, painful to producers of import substitutes, who find their domestic market inundated with products sold by foreign competitors. Adjustment from a deficit position calls for a reduction in imports painful to consumers who are getting too poor to afford the imported goods or who find these goods becoming too expensive to buy; and it calls for an increase in exports, painful to both consumers and producers, consumers because they have to give up buying domestic products which they can no longer afford with their reduced incomes or at the increased prices, producers because the loss of business in the domestic markets forces them to find less attractive foreign outlets for their goods.

Since adjustment—real adjustment in the form of a reallocation of real resources—hurts, it is resisted by all who have power to resist it. But this resistance means for a deficit country that it continues overspending by using up its foreign assets or by incurring more

---

*The effects of inflation on relative prices, because of unavoidable differences in reaction times and in price flexibilities—the distortion of the price structure—will be discussed more in detail in the second lecture.

foreign debts. For a surplus country it means that the country continues to use an excessive part of its productive resources for piling up unwanted foreign assets instead of letting its own people enjoy the increases in consumption and domestic investment that they could have on the basis of their productive capacity.

Thus, whereas adjustment hurts, nonadjustment or delayed adjustment may eventually hurt even more. More often than not, the delay may inflict serious injury upon the economy. With these observations on the resistance to adjustment and on the consequences of postponing it we have made the transition to the theme of the second lecture, the problem of timing. The main question will concern the comparative risks of hasty, premature action, on the one hand, and of hesitation and delay, on the other.

NOTES

1. Reprinted in Machlup, Fritz, ed., *Essays in Economic Semantics* (New York: W. W. Norton, 1967).

2. Included in Richard E. Caves, Harry G. Johnson and Peter B. Kenen, eds. *Trade, Growth and the Balance of Payments* (Chicago: Rand McNally and Co., and Amsterdam: North-Holland Publishing Co., 1965), pp. 185-213.

3. *Balance-of-Payments Adjustments Policies: Japan, Germany and the Netherlands* (New York: distributed by Columbia University Press for the National Bureau of Economic Research, 1968).

4. Published in Fellner, Wm., et al., *Maintaining and Restoring Balance in International Payments* (Princeton: Princeton University Press, 1966).

The major conclusion of my first lecture was that, under the most likely conditions, adjustment of exchange rates is the least-cost method of restoring balance in foreign payments, less costly than selective measures on particular transactions and less costly than adjustment of aggregate demand. From the large number of exchange-rate adjustments in the last twenty-five years one might draw the inference that countries have found out that this is the least troublesome and least injurious method. Yet, to conclude from the frequency of a governmental measure that it is the wisest, the best of all possibilities, would be rather naive. After all, most governments, before they decided to adjust the disaligned exchange rates of their currencies, adopted all sorts of restrictions and direct controls in the hope that they could thereby avoid the adjustment of exchange rates. The number of restrictions and quantitative controls introduced in many countries was undoubtedly much greater than the number of exchange-rate adjustments, but no sane and informed person could infer that these selective measures were helpful to anybody but small groups with special interests.

The costly and usually ineffective selective correctives were adopted in the hope that exchange-rate adjustment could thereby be averted. These hopes were eventually disappointed and exchange-rate adjustments became imperative. Of course, aggregate-demand adjustments were always recommended and advertised as the most virtuous of the alternative restorers of balance, but virtue is often a luxury which a nation cannot afford or is unwilling to pay for; only in a few cases did monetary authorities follow through with monetary and fiscal policies sufficiently strong to restore external balance. What happened most frequently was that the men in charge of monetary and financial affairs *talked* about adjusting aggregate demand to given exchange rates, *actually* imposed restrictions and controls on specific kinds of transactions in international trade and finance, and *ended up* adjusting the exchange rates when this seemed the only way out. A review of the approximately 250 adjustments of exchange rates during the 25-year period—almost all *de*valuations—reveals that most of them came too late. They were resisted till the bitter end.

Our main tasks in this second lecture are to inquire into the reasons for the resistance to realignment of exchange rates, to sort out the defensible from the indefensible reasons, and to examine whether there is something like the "best time for action." If realignment is indicated as the best remedy, what is the best time for it? What are the chances for the realignment to be too early or too late and what are the costs of being too early or too late? The problem of optimal timing will be our major concern.

RESISTANCE TO CHANGING THE EXCHANGE RATES

There was a time when the majority of academic specialists firmly supported a system of unalterable exchange rates as the most appropriate arrangement for international trade and payments. This was the time before nations embraced national objectives the attainment of which is often incompatible with unchanging exchange rates. In the last thirty years, academic opinion has been unanimous in its support of adjustable rates. Adjustability was provided in the Articles of Agreement which established the International Monetary Fund. When many countries refused to make use of these provisions and tried to defend disaligned rates by all sorts of selective restrictions, academic economists began to speak out for greater flexibility. Some would be satisfied with the original provisions if they were used with less delay; some want adoption of freely flexible rates, neither limited in their variations nor managed by official interventions; and a third group, probably the majority, want provisions and practices which encourage gliding adjustments, by limited variations, to repair disalignments before they become serious.

We shall not at this point deal with the *academic* discussion about frequent and small adjustments versus infrequent and large ones. We are interested now in the *political* resistance to exchange-rate adjustments, even if some of the resisters and objectors draw on academic arguments in support of their position.

Why They Oppose Adjustments in Either Direction

While some of the political resistance is to upvaluation of the currency in surplus countries and some is to devaluation in deficit countries, there are several reasons that militate against any adjustment, up or down. These shall be reviewed first.

Fear of Change

The most general reason for resisting realignment is the plain and simple fear of change. Even some of those who are unhappy with a given situation may fear change more than continuation of the unsatisfactory conditions. Sometimes the fears are rationalized and the "dire consequences" of change spelled out; but often the fears remain unspecified, as in the warning "There will be chaos." Against phobias of this sort rational argument may be of little avail.

Moral Principle

Appeals to moral principles are quite customary in this context. Once up a time the gold standard was regarded as "good" and paper currency as "evil"; in direct descendance from this moral judgment, unchanging exchange rates are sometimes regarded as good and changing rates as evil. With proper monetary discipline changes in exchange rates can be avoided; it is then taken to be self-evident that lack of discipline is immoral, and discipline (even if it causes mass unemployment) is moral. Thus, there are still many—in high finance, if not in government—who see exchange-rate realignment as a violation of a moral principle: "It's a bad thing and ought not to be done!" I find it difficult to see why the maintenance of fixed exchange rates should be "morally superior" to that of stable price levels or high rates of employment; but I know that arguments on morality are seldom very fruitful.

Elasticity Pessimism

Twenty years ago, I coined this expression to refer to the possibility that the elasticities of supply and demand in the market for foreign exchange are terribly low or even perverse. If they are terribly low, a change in exchange rates would fail to improve an existing imbalance; if they are perverse, equilibrium in the market would be unstable and any change in exchange rates would lead to explosive deteriorations of the imbalance. In either case, the pessimists would say about proposals for realignment that "It won't work." Elasticity pessimism was once respectable in academic discussion; it stopped being so when improved tools of empirical analysis allowed better estimates. But among practical men elasticity pessimism is always strong and pervasive—producers minimizing the effect of prices on the demand for their products, labor leaders minimizing the effect of wage rates on the demand for labor, central bankers the effect of interest rates on the demand for loans, and finance ministers the effect of exchange rates on the demand for foreign exchange.

Hope for Reversal

Perhaps the most common reason for resisting adjustment of exchange rates is the hope that it will turn out to be unnecessary. In the minds of many this is not merely a pious hope but a firm expectation based on supposedly realistic assumptions. The assumptions may either be regarding the reversal of trends or developments that have led to the imbalance or regarding the effectiveness of government measures designed to produce a reversal. Sometimes the strongest expectations rest on the flimsiest arguments, such as the "sure" success of an export drive, the probability of better crops, the non-recurrence of industrial work stoppages. Often the expectations rest on the belief that certain selective restrictions will reduce the imbalance of payments and not, through repercussions and feedbacks, some other items that are among the transactions entered "above the line." With all these hopes and expectations, the sanguine resisters of exchange-rate adjustment say "It won't be necessary." If we collected all the public statements of the responsible officials—presidents, prime ministers, finance ministers, governors, and all the rest—about the impending removal of imbalance, about the restoration of balance "next year," we would find that 95 per cent of the confident predictions were proven false by actual events.

Why They Oppose Adjustments Upward

The four reasons for resisting adjustments which we have reviewed thus far are employed with equal fervor against upvaluations and against devaluations. Resistance against upvaluations is particularly strong, as may be inferred from the fact that only three of the approximately 250 exchange-rate adjustments in the last 25 years were in the upward direction.

Since the sum total of surpluses is always greater than the sum total of deficits in the balance of payments (on the basis of changes in official reserves), surpluses are evidently not considered to be as serious imbalances as deficits. A good many countries have had surpluses for several years in a row but regarded the continuous increase in reserves as something normal and desirable. With regular annual increases in world reserves in the form of gold or special drawing rights it would be conceivable for all countries to have surpluses with no country having a deficit. Only surpluses in excess of the rate of increase in nondebt world reserves would be indicative of deficits by other countries and hence, of nonsustainable imbalances in international payments. Put differently, surpluses which could not exist if other countries did not have deficits qualify as imbalances that could not go on forever and, hence, call for adjustment. If this adjustment does not come by means of inflation in the surplus countries and/or unemployment in the deficit countries, it can come only by way of a realignment of exchange rates. The realignment may be through devaluation by the deficit countries or through upvaluation by the surplus countries. If these changes in valuation are in terms of the U.S. dollar as a standard currency, it depends on the payments balance of the United States which of the two possible par value changes is preferable. If the United States were in surplus, world-wide balance would require devaluations by deficit countries. If the United States is in deficit, world-wide balance requires upvaluations by surplus countries.

Considerations of this sort are still novel and not widely understood. They are presented here chiefly in order to show that upvaluations ought not to be regarded as very unusual, exceptional moves. With the United States in perennial deficit in amounts larger than the desired increases in dollar reserves held by the rest of the world, the presumption is in favor of adjustment by means of increases in the external values of the currencies of countries in persistent surplus. Yet, upvaluation is resisted strongly, even in the face of reserve accumulations at abnormally high rates, of export surpluses clearly excessive relative to gross national product, and of price inflation at rates far above the acceptable. Here are some of the reasons that inspire resistance.

The Others' Fault

The governments and monetary authorities of surplus countries often feel self-righteous about the monetary and fiscal discipline that has secured them their "favorable" international position and strong currency, while other countries have evidently indulged in lax policies leading to overspending, price inflation, and deficits. Surely, it is the fault of these spendthrift nations if their currencies have become overvalued, and it is up to them to realign their exchange rates. Why should the surplus countries have to act if the undervaluation of their currencies is the consequence of the overindulgence of the others? "Why should we pay for the others' lack of discipline?" ask the political, financial, and industrial leaders of the surplus country. The unwillingness to take the consequences of a situation caused by others is as smart as to refuse to avoid a collision with another automobile because it is on the wrong side of the highway or because it failed to recognize your right of way. Even if the "wrong policies" of the other countries have caused the imbalance, the surplus country will only at its peril refuse to realign its exchange rate.

The Others' Gain

Closely related to the unwillingness to upvalue because the undervaluation has been the fault of other countries is the resistance to upvaluation on the ground that it would be a favor to the deficit countries, making things easier for them. The politicians opposing upvaluation ask "Why should we do a favor to others at great expense to ourselves?" The error lies in the idea that the upvaluation would be at the expense of the surplus country. If it reduces an excessive export surplus to the size commensurate to the normal capital outflow and to the share of the national product and the national savings that the country desires to invest abroad rather than at home, the revaluation that ends the undervaluation of the currency is entirely in the national interest.

Loss of Exports

Usually the strongest argument against upvaluation is the loss of exports that it would cause. It is so strong because the interests of a powerful group, the export industries, are at stake. The two previous arguments are merely ideological; in contrast, the campaign of the export producers is inspired by self-interest and financed to protect their own incomes and the incomes of their employees. In fighting the upvaluation, they fight a reduction of the proceeds from export sales, they fight to defend their investment in export capacity and to keep their export markets, which they may have built up at great expense. "We would no longer be competitive and would lose our export markets," is their outcry, which may be quite correct in stating the consequences of the realignment of exchange rates. Yet, the interests of the export sector are not necessarily identical with the national interest. If the export surplus is excessive, largely because of the undervaluation of the currency in the foreign-exchange market, a paring of the exports may be precisely the adjustment that the nation needs.

More Competition from Imports

Only slightly less vocal may be the resistance movement which the import-competing industries organize against any plans to upvalue the currency. Imports would become cheaper, foreign competition would become stronger. The threatened industrialists cry out: "Our home market would be inundated by cheap imports!" And, of course, this may be true—and consumers could rejoice. The increase in imports may be just what the nation needs.

Braking the Boom

The reduction of the export surplus (or increase of an import surplus) that would result from an upvaluation may easily have deflationary or, rather, disinflationary effects. Thus, one may hear complaints that "The economy would be slowed down and unemployment would increase." If the surplus has been associated with imported inflation and an overheated economy, a cooling-down as a result of stopping the surplus may be the right prescription. Any related decline in the demand for labor may be merely an alleviation of a condition of overemployment and of the wage and profit inflation that is usually linked with it.

Why They Oppose Adjustments Downward

The case for and against upvaluation may strike many in my audience as uninteresting, because it is so completely irrelevant to the position of their country. But we now come to the case for and against devaluation, and this they may find a more timely subject of discussion. What with the long record of debates in the many countries that have devalued after long delays and in some countries that are still delaying devaluations long since overdue, we have to deal with a larger list of reasons for resistance.

The Nation's Honor and Prestige

In at least one country devaluation was resisted because it was regarded as a stain or blemish on the nation's honor and renown. Strangely enough, that proud nation had devalued previously more often than any other financially advanced country. Resistance to devaluation because it would lower the prestige of the nation has not been confined, however, to de Gaulle's France; it has probably been a weighty consideration in the opposition to devaluation on the part of some political leaders of several countries. "The honor of the nation forbids us to debase its currency," is their parole. Yet, the act of devaluation is only the acknowledgement of an accomplished fact, of a disalignment which may or may not have been the consequence of faulty policies. To pursue policies leading to an overvaluation of the currency may possibly be deemed dishonorable (though even this only by somewhat Puritan standards), but to recognize what has happened and to be forthright about it is anything but dishonorable.

Failure and Dismissal

A very strong reason for a finance minister or the entire cabinet to resist devaluation is that this action is widely regarded as an admission of defeat, or failure, if not malfeasance. The financial and monetary policies of the past have led to an imbalance; if this imbalance is not merely temporary but has to be dealt with by devaluation of the currency, then, clearly, these past policies must have been "wrong." To admit this will mean, in all probability, that "We shall be thrown out." This is true whether it is a parliamentary democracy that may vote the government out of office, whether the ruling party has to fear that the voters will not return it to power at the next election, or whether it is only the minister of finance who has to resign or will be dismissed to allow another man to do a better job. All these fears are firmly based on experience, as Richard Cooper has established by political statistics. He has examined the frequency of governments or finance ministers losing office within one year after devaluation and found that the probability of governments falling doubles and of finance ministers being dismissed trebles.[1] This may be as strong a reason for resisting devaluation as any—though it does not make its postponement any less injurious to the nation.

The Terms of Trade

Consequences for the nation as a whole, say, for the size of the national income, are less likely to carry much political weight, especially if they are difficult to understand, almost impossible to make intelligible to the voters, and quite impossible to prove. Still, among the reasons for resisting devaluation one sometimes hears the assertion that "National income would be reduced by a worsening of the terms of trade." The idea is that the ratio of prices received for export to prices paid for imports may decline as a result of higher prices being paid for foreign currencies. Whether devaluation actually will have this effect is by no means certain; and if it has, the resulting loss of income will be too small to worry about. It is a fine point of economic theory, and theorists love to argue about it. But it is not an issue about which politicians can or should get excited.

Distribution of Income

Effects upon the distribution of income do sometimes become political issues, particularly where political parties claim to represent the interests of groups whose share in the national income may be reduced by proposed government measures. Devaluation, as a rule, will increase the prices of imports and of exportables, and if these products include many consumer goods, the buying power of the workers, or of the masses, may be reduced. Politicians are apt to take up the cudgels in behalf of the groups with the largest numbers of votes and, thus, to campaign against devaluation because "It would cut the spending power of the masses." If payments deficits indicate overspending and if overspending has to be terminated, one will be hard put to solve the problem of how to stop overspending without reducing the spending power of those who do most of the spending.

Serving External Debt

There is an argument peculiar to countries that have large external debts, especially public debt, denominated in foreign currency. As devaluation implies a higher price for foreign currency, the cost in domestic money of serving these foreign debts will be increased. If the debt service is a considerable portion of the government's budget, the finance minister will resist devaluation because "It would increase the burden of the foreign debt and unbalance the budget." The minister is quite right in that he may have the difficult task of increasing the tax revenue or of cutting other expenditures, but he is wrong if he believes that he has a valid reason for opposing the realignment of exchange rates. His problem is not any worse than that of any other person or group that has to adjust. The necessary changes in the government's budget are part of the inevitable end to national overspending.

The Jobs of the Exchange Controllers

The power of vested interests is often overestimated, but sometimes it is applied so subtly and discreetly that outsiders fail to recognize it. Among the groups who have a vested interest in continued overvaluation of the currency are the employees in exchange-control departments or agencies, usually attached to the central bank, the ministry of finance or commerce, or to other public or mixed organizations. A devaluation that removes the overvaluation endangers the jobs of the exchange controllers, since no such controls are needed if the currency is correctly priced in the foreign-exchange markets. The staying power of the exchange-control staff is sometimes strong enough to survive all balance-of-payments difficulties and to stay on the job many years after its original function has vanished. But one cannot always count on the extraordinary inertia of the bureaucracy and it seems safer to resist devaluation since "It would destroy the usefulness of exchange control." If one doubts that a group of such small size could exercise any power, let us remember that its members are credited with having special expertise in matters of foreign exchange.

The Opportunities of Planners

Every government includes enthusiasts for central economic planning. Exchange controls afford the planners opportunities which they are denied in a free-market economy. With exchange controls, they have to decide which imports are more important, less important, or superfluous; how much of each commodity ought to be allowed into the country; and which firms should get permission to import. Every one of these decisions is a part of economic planning and the planners feel very important, very patriotic, and very powerful. This central economic planning via import licenses is seen as a stage on the way to comprehensive planning of the entire economy, and this again increases the importance of the activity. Devaluation, however, could restore balance in foreign payments, and could remove the need for exchange controls. Thus, "It could destroy the chances for planning," and ought to be resisted, lest free competition replace the sound judgment of the authorities.

The Protection of Monopolists

Another group with special interests in the maintenance of exchange controls consists of producers potentially exposed to competition from abroad. It may seem strange that they should resist devaluation, since a higher price for foreign currency would increase the prices of imports and thereby improve the competitiveness of the domestic products. Yet, these producers are much better protected by the scarcity of import licenses under a system of exchange controls. The foreign prices, however low they appear to be at the existing exchange rate, are ineffective if the foreign goods, because of the scarcity of foreign exchange, are not allowed into the country. Add to this protection from foreign competition, the virtual elimination of domestic competition which is implied in the rationing of foreign exchange for the import of any materials or intermediate goods that may be needed by the industry, and it becomes clear that there is a vested interest in continuing the overvaluation of the currency and the controls that this necessitates. Hence, here is another reason for resisting devaluation, for "It would reduce the protection of import-competing producers." It goes without saying that, from the point of view of the economic welfare of the nation as a whole, this would be all to the good.

The Acceleration of Price Inflation

Probably the most serious reason for resisting devaluation is the probability that devaluation will accelerate a price inflation that has been going on despite efforts to control it. As the price of foreign currency is increased, prices of imports and of exportables will be increased in domestic money. Some of the imports are ingredients in domestic production, so that production costs rise in many industries. Moreover, the rise in the cost of living will lead to demands for higher wages by trade unions, perhaps even to some automatic wage increases under previously agreed escalation clauses. The increased labor cost would soon be reflected in higher product prices all around. Thus, it is said that "The wage-price spiral would run up at a steeper rate." It is possible to reject this argument by insisting on very orthodox monetary assumptions: strict control of the money stock could prevent the speed-up of price inflation. However, can one reasonably expect that the policy makers have the political courage to keep the supply of credit and money in check sufficiently to hold aggregate demand and prices down despite the pressure of rising costs? The argument is too important to be dealt with in one paragraph. We shall have to come back to it, after we present two other reasons for resisting devaluation, which will likewise call for special consideration.

The Right Moment

It sometimes happens that the men in charge of monetary and financial policy agree in private and in strict secrecy that an existing payments deficit is a symptom of a disalignment that calls for adjustment of the exchange rate. Yet they hold that the time is not right to act immediately and that one must wait for the "right moment." The criteria, however, of what is the right and what is a wrong time to devalue the currency vary from person to person. Some merely want to wait until speculation subsides and people no longer expect the inevitable to happen soon. Others believe that certain preconditions must be fulfilled before D-day, chiefly a state of fiscal austerity and stern monetary discipline; they believe, in other words, that devaluation would be premature as long as monetary expansion continues. Some want to wait until the next round of wage increases has been completed, and others until the current balance of payments shows signs of improvement. We shall have to return to this claim that "We must wait for the right moment."

The Big Shock

The recommendation of frequent and small adjustments of the exchange rate, instead of infrequent and large realignments, is opposed in some quarters on the ground that small changes, even a series of small changes, would have no effect on the flow of goods and services. Only large changes could be effective, because it takes a big push with its shock effect upon business to redirect productive resources into different uses. Hence, it is argued, it would be useless to adjust exchange rates gradually, in small steps; it is better to wait until the disalignment is big enough to require a large change for realignment: "Only abrupt, drastic changes are effective." This is the third argument to be examined at greater length.

Devaluation and the Rate of Price Inflation

As devaluation increases the prices of imports and of exportables, it promotes cost-push inflation as well as demand-pull inflation, the former because the monetary authorities will not refuse the "supportive" expansion of the money stock (needed to maintain employment), the latter because they will not refuse to meet the induced demand for additional credit. The question is whether the likelihood that it may accelerate the price inflation justifies postponing or opposing devaluation.

Stability of the price level, measured by an appropriate price index, is an important national objective, but not an ultimate goal. An increase in the price index is objectionable because certain effects upon national income and its distribution are ordinarily associated with the process of price inflation. The effects on distribution can conceivably be offset by redistributive fiscal policy, taxing those who gain and compensating those who lose as a result of the inequitable effects of the inflation. The effects on the size of the national product, however, cannot be repaired and the shortfalls are lost forever. What causes these losses?

If all prices of all goods and services were to increase at the same time by the same percentage, production would not be affected. If, however, the rates of price increase are different for different goods and services, some prices rising faster, others more slowly, and some seriously falling behind, the allocation of productive resources will be affected, and the presumption is that it will be unfavorably affected. In other words, the process of inflation involves a distortion of the price structure, leading to a misallocation of resources. The resulting loss in efficiency of production implies a loss of output.

Slowing down the rate of price inflation will reduce the loss of output if the retardation reduces the price distortion, but it will increase the loss of output if it increases the differences in the rates of increase. If the rate of increase of the price index is kept lower by keeping some prices from rising at all or from rising as fast as other prices, the price distortion is made worse. Holding down some prices *may* achieve a retardation of the *average* rate of price increase—I said "may," not "will," because it is quite possible that other prices will rise faster when the money that does not have to be spent on the low-priced goods is available for buying more of other things. But even if the average rate of price increase is reduced by price stops, price ceilings, or other devices, the differences in relative price increases are thereby increased, and with them the misallocation of resources.

This is precisely what the well-meaning "controllers of inflation" achieve: They make the economic cost of a 5 per cent price inflation higher than the cost of an uncontrolled 10 per cent inflation would be.

One of the worst distorters of the price structure is an unchanged foreign-exchange rate in the midst of increases of all sorts of domestic costs and prices. By keeping the exchange rate pegged at an unchanged level, imported goods are held down while the prices of many domestic products increase; export products, likewise, fetch unchanged prices in domestic money while their production costs and the prices in domestic markets are increased. If the price of foreign currency were currently adjusted, so that the rate of price increase of imports and exportables were commensurate to that of goods not internationally traded, the average rate of price inflation might be higher but the degree of price distortion would be lower. The economic cost of the accelerated inflation would be lower than that of the slower inflation at disaligned exchange rates.

These considerations may not impress those who are in constant fear of cost push through excessive wage escalation. Yet, there is little evidence that wages have been more often or more effectively pushed up by aggressive labor unions than pulled up by demand expansion fed by lax monetary policy. Moreover, the same wage demands that are made on the ground of increases in the cost of living would be based on other arguments if the living cost had not increased. After all, if wages were raised only when, and by no more than, consumer prices had risen, wage-push inflation would peter out in most countries.

Those who fear the effects of devaluation upon price indexes should also be reminded of the fact that, if devaluation comes after a delay during which imports have been restricted by direct controls, these quantitative restrictions may have had their effects on prices. Their replacement by an undisguised increase in the price of foreign currency would not always raise prices.

If a postponement of devaluation slows down the price inflation temporarily, it may aggravate it in the longer run. Holding-down of the prices of imports and of exportables may for a while keep the price index from rising as fast as it would with gliding adjustments of exchange rates. Sooner or later, however, it will prove impossible to defer devaluation any longer—and the delayed devaluation will be, as a rule, by a substantially larger percentage, and will raise prices to a level higher than they would have reached with gradual adjustment. In other words, by keeping prices of imports, exportables, and goods related to them, a little lower during the period of "successful postponement," governments succeed only in holding the price index down for a period of price distortion and then letting it catch up in a hurry. The price inflation is thus not reduced *over time*. The postponement will have been costly without having served a good purpose.

We conclude that it is unsound to oppose devaluation on the ground that it would accelerate price inflation. The feared acceleration would, in fact, reduce price distortion and thus reduce the chief economic cost of inflation.

Waiting for the Right Moment

Most of the things for which the authorities say they must wait before they can devalue are not worth discussing. One argument for postponement, however, deserves careful consideration: that it is wrong to devalue while the economy is overheated, that one should wait until the economy has been cooled down, so that devaluation will not add fuel to the flames.

If it is only the end of a money inflation that defines the right moment for adjusting the currency's external value in the foreign-exchange market, one must realize that this moment never comes all by itself, but is the result of resolute action by the monetary and fiscal authorities. If such action has been taken and is expected to have the desired effect within a few weeks, then the explanation is credible and the postponement by a month or two is reasonable. However, if the action, say, a large tax increase to balance the government's budget, is only intended, or is planned for next year, or even for the next half-year, then postponement of devaluation or depreciation of the currency is not warranted. The increasing distortion of the price structure during the waiting period will cost the nation dearly and the delay of the exchange-rate adjustment will have been of no use.

If monetary and demand expansion goes on at a rate far exceeding the rates of expansion abroad, the exchange rate ought to be currently adjusted. If the expansion is eventually stopped (or decelerated to the pace prevailing in the countries with which most of the country's trade is conducted), another adjustment, perhaps a final adjustment after a series of provisional adjustments, may be called for. No sound argument supports the idea that exchange rates should not be allowed to adjust while money supply, aggregate demand, prices of domestically produced goods, and wage rates continue to increase. Price inflation, especially trotting and galloping inflation, is bad in any case, but with exchange rates kept unchanged it is much worse.

The Shock Theory

The theory that small changes in exchange rates have no effect on the allocation of productive resources and on the international flows of goods and services has been advanced by several practitioners and supported by a few economic theorists. Strangely enough, some practitioners contradict one another, and even themselves, as they hold at the same time that even slight variations of exchange rates—for example, within a widened band around parity—can destroy the foreign markets of certain industries or even destroy those industries altogether. We shall not exploit these contradictions, but shall subject the theory of the ineffectiveness of small exchange-rate adjustments to a fair examination.

If correct, the theory could justify resistance against frequent and small adjustments of exchange rates and support infrequent but sizable adjustments. But why should five consecutive devaluations by 2 per cent each have less effect upon production and trade than a single devaluation by 10 or 11 per cent? One possible answer would be that there is usually enough slack in the operations of a firm to absorb a small increase in cost or reduction in proceeds without forcing the management to redirect its resources or outputs. If the next change in cost or proceeds comes only after some time, say, after a year, the firm will again be able to absorb it and not be forced to react by transferring inputs to new activities or outputs to new markets. In contrast, a change in cost or proceeds by an amount five times larger could not help having a drastic effect on the dispositions of any firm.

Another answer follows more psychological lines: large changes often have traumatic effects while small changes are hardly felt. Thus, it takes shock effects to make managers of business respond to changes in conditions. A devaluation by 10 per cent or more can have shock effects; a devaluation by 1 or 2 per cent would do nothing to the use of real resources.

There is no direct empirical evidence either way and one cannot deny that the theory which indicates the need of shock therapy has a ring of plausibility. It rests, however, on an assumption which is not tenable, namely, that economic changes will have consequences only if they affect all or almost all decision-makers. To be sure, it would be quite unreasonable to expect everybody to react to every change, but it is equally unreasonable to believe that universal reaction is required for economic effects to materialize. If one or two out of a hundred firms react in the ways depicted by economic theory, this suffices for the inferred outcome to be effected. The reactions by the marginal seller, the marginal buyer, the marginal producer, the marginal consumer, are all that is needed. The elasticity of demand, for example, is not zero even if most buyers fail to notice the change in price or, if they notice it, fail to adjust the quantities they purchase; responses by a few "at the margin" are enough for elasticity to be non-zero.

To admit that a shock may be needed to make *everybody* jump is not to accept the shock theory of economic adjustment, since only the responses of a few in each area of activity are required. I doubt that even the believers in economic shock therapy will contend that *nobody* is sensitive enough to react to small changes. I conclude that the shock theory does not justify postponing realignments of the exchange rate until they have to be big enough to shock everybody.

OBJECTIONS TO GREATER FLEXIBILITY

In the first part of this lecture the reasons for resisting exchange-rate adjustments were reviewed. These were chiefly the reasons that cause the men in power and those of influence to oppose particular changes in the value at which their currency is traded in the foreign-exchange market. When such changes, upward or downward, are suggested or recommended they say "no" or "not now"; their resistance leads regularly to much larger changes later.

Economists who know that delays in adjustment are wasteful and that large adjustments cause unnecessary disruption have for years recommended that exchange rates be realigned without delay and by smaller changes. Their plea for a system that facilitates and encourages smaller and more frequent changes in exchange rates has been accompanied by a variety of recommendations. These have ranged from appeals to greater obedience to the IMF Articles of Agreement—which call for adjustment in case of fundamental disequilibrium—to widening the range or "band" within which exchange rates may respond to market forces, to permitting more continuous and gradual adjustment of parities, and to allowing freely floating exchange rates either for limited periods of transition or for indefinite periods.

The plea for greater flexibility has met with varying response. There has been much understanding and support from men in high positions in the monetary system, including several central bankers.

But there has been also a good deal of opposition. The arguments of the opposition to a system of greater flexibility of exchange rates will now be considered.

An Invitation to Financial Intemperance

Perhaps the most widely professed argument against greater flexibility of exchange rates is that governments, especially finance ministers and central bankers, will more readily indulge in fiscal extravagance and monetary softness if they do not have to fear that the country's foreign reserves will be depleted. Only a loss of reserves can impress them with the threat which a continuation of easy money would involve. If a reduction in the external value of the currency becomes an acceptable thing—perhaps an annual affair or one recurring even more frequently—the men in charge of the government's budget or in control of bank credit will have no restraining discipline and no hold or bar enabling them to stand fast against the easy spenders and lenders.

The feared or dreaded consequences of a depletion of reserves would be that the exchange rate of the currency could no longer be pegged and would therefore decline in the market. How strange that a loss of reserves should be an effective deterrent but a decline in the exchange rate should fail to deter the monetary authorities! Yet, several ministers and governors say that this is actually the present situation in their countries. It is not so everywhere, according to some ministers and governors who have testified that the poor or healthy state of reserves does not impress their countrymen either as a warning against or an inducement for the pursuit of expansionary policies.

There was a time when gains and losses of reserves were virtually the only guides for monetary policy; the notion that nothing but losses of reserves will keep the authorities from overexpanding domestic bank credit is apparently an inheritance from that time. Monetary policy in most countries has long since accepted other guides, some perhaps rather unwisely; in any case, not many countries are left in which actual or feared losses of reserves are necessary and sufficient conditions for the pursuit of non-inflationary policies. There are countries in which perennial budget deficits are financed by the central bank, regardless of the state of monetary reserves. In other countries certain objectives regarding economic growth, development, employment, or national security are pursued with the aid of monetary expansion and without serious inhibitions on account of monetary reserves. And in a good many countries the objective of price-level stability, or avoidance of too-fast-creeping price inflation, is the main restraining force in monetary policy, a force neither weakened by inflows nor strengthened by outflows of reserves.

Reliance on fear of reserve depletion as chief deterrent of monetary overexpansion has the very serious disadvantage that governments resort to selective restrictions and direct controls in order to avoid reserve losses. If their aim is to avoid losing reserves, they can succeed in this by suppressing some or all of the excess demand for foreign currency that results from the overexpansion of aggregate demand in the country. As a result they will have the worst of all possible combinations: They will not have avoided the inflation of demand and domestic prices, they will have created a distortion of the price structure, and they will control and restrict foreign trade and capital movements.

There is no doubt that fiscal and monetary discipline is needed to safeguard stable growth in the economy. This discipline, however, should be oriented on other criteria than the state of monetary reserves with fixed and often seriously disaligned exchange rates. The objection to current gliding realignments of exchange rates on the ground that they remove the discipline enforced by the fear of reserve losses cannot reasonably be sustained.

The Danger of Competitive Devaluation

In the bad depression years of the 1930s several countries resorted to competitive devaluations, by which they tried to "export" their unemployment to their trading partners. One country after another reduced the foreign price of its currency in order to make its products more competitive abroad and exchange them for foreign money; it thereby created more domestic money and jobs for its masses of unemployed, but at the same time imposed payments deficits, deflation, and unemployment upon other countries. This bad practice was appropriately called a "beggar-my-neighbor policy." One of the important principles of the IMF Articles of Agreement was to prevent recurrence of this practice by forbidding member countries to change the par values of their currencies by more than 10 per cent from the initially established ones, except in instances of fundamental disequilibrium recognized by the Executive Directors of the Fund.

If this prohibition is now abolished and greater flexibility of exchange rates is permitted, are we not inviting the practice of competitive devaluation to return? It would depend, of course, on just what system of limited flexibility is adopted. There are different types of flexibility: the new provisions may, for example, (a) widen the margin within which the monetary authorities of a country may without intervening allow the exchange rate of its currency to deviate from par solely as a result of free-market forces (a "wider band"), (b) allow countries to determine a new, slightly different parity or pegging level (intervention price) on the basis of a formula agreed on or stipulated in advance (a "formula-determined crawl of the peg"), (c) allow countries to determine a new pegging level without fixed formula but only after consultation or negotiation with the Fund, or (d) allow countries to determine a new slightly different pegging level at their own discretion. Only the fourth alternative includes a possibility of competitive devaluation.

It is deplorable if men in high positions in banking and finance confuse issues by sloppy use of language. Some ministers and governors have been heard denouncing "freely floating exchange rates" as involving the danger of "competitive devaluation." Devaluation is a change of a fixed rate, but a floating rate is the opposite of a fixed one. If rates are allowed to float, a currency may depreciate whenever market forces move it that way, but it cannot be devalued. Competititve devaluation is an intentional change in the rate fixed by the monetary authorities in opposition to market forces, cheapening the currency by means of official purchases of foreign exchange at prices which the free market would not pay. If monetary authorities are not free to purchase foreign currencies at prices raised at their discretion, competitive devaluation is ruled out.

A widening of the band around parity cannot be used for competitive cheapening of the currency if the authorities are not permitted to intervene within the band; it can be so used if they intervene by purchasing foreign exchange at or close to the highest price allowed by the band, a price at which they are supposed to sell, not buy, foreign exchange. There can be no competitive devaluation if changes in par values are determined by a formula stipulated in advance; but since it is not easy to come up with a formula that is acceptable, this form of limited flexibility is unlikely to be adopted. Changes in par values and exchange rates by consultation with the Fund would hardly be of the competitive type, so harmful to other countries. Only discretionary flexibility could be misused for competitive devaluation; but, if the Articles of Agreement are revised to make rates more flexible, the national authorities need not be given completely free rein. The revised provisions may still include safeguards against competitive devaluation.

In discussing safeguards against bad practice, we are taking the talk about the danger of competitive devaluations far more seriously than it deserves. The men who raise warning fingers about this danger forget that the world has changed since the 1930s and that policies to raise employment levels are no longer quite so primitive as they were then. In those years it was believed that it was very bad to increase aggregate spending by money creation through expanding the domestic assets of the banking system, but quite all right to increase it through purchasing foreign assets. To pay higher prices for foreign currency was thought to be the only safe way of stimulating economic activity. Nowadays, expansionary fiscal and monetary policies are the preferred instruments in attaining high-employment targets, and few governments, if any, propose to use devaluation as their chief or only method of reducing unemployment. The last 25 years have shown that governments have shied away from devaluation even when it was needed to realign exchange rates that were badly overvalued; in no country has devaluation been proposed with the intent of producing artificially an undervaluation of the currency for the purpose of stimulating employment through larger exports and reduced imports.

We conclude that the fear that greater flexibility of exchange rates would bring back the practice of competitive devaluation is not justified.

A Handicap to Foreign Trade and Investment

One of the most widely accepted objections to greater flexibility of exchange rates rests on the belief that it would increase the risks and costs of foreign trade and foreign investment and thereby reduce the international flows of goods, services, and long-term capital.

This belief can be broken down into several separate propositions: first, that greater flexibility will mean wider variations and greater instability of exchange rates; second, that greater variations of exchange rates will depress foreign trade and investment; and third, that where variations of rates are avoided and fixed rates maintained this is done without governmental restrictions and direct controls of foreign trade and capital flows. All three propositions must be questioned. The first two can be held bona fide, but the third is so patently contrary to fact that it would suggest disingenousness if one were not sure of the honest naiveté of those who hold it. As long as governments restrict foreign trade and investment in order to keep exchange rates invariant, it is surely illegitimate to argue that variable rates would reduce trade and investment.

The first proposition cannot be proved or disproved on the basis of our present knowledge. Some hold that rates would be more stable in the long run if they were more flexibile in the short run; they believe that delay in the adjustment of exchange rates allows disequilibrating forces to build up to greater strength, forcing in the end a more drastic change than the sum of small alterations would have been. The opponents of greater flexibility believe the opposite; they hold that the sum of small steps would be greater than the one big step that eventually becomes inevitable if the country does not resort to restrictions and direct controls. They point to the ratchet effects of frequent small devaluations—wage escalations making it difficult ever to reverse any movement in the exchange rate—and to the expansionary effects of delayed upvaluations—imported inflations reducing the need for exchange-rate adjustment. No empirical evidence is available to decide the argument.

The second proposition has been accepted as self-evident, but the experience of the last 25 years should induce us to challenge it.

Repeated references to the Bretton Woods system as a system of fixed exchange rates have led many to believe that the last 25 years were actually a period of relatively invariant exchange rates. In fact, however, the number of exchange-rate alterations was greater than in any comparable period in international monetary history. Yet, the volume of international trade and the volume of international capital movements increased at faster rates than ever before. This increase was probably due to liberalization—the abolition of quotas, the reduction of tariffs, and the removal or relaxation of restrictions on payments and capital movements—largely thanks to the fast growth of the monetary reserves of most countries as a result of the almost continuous payments deficits of the United States from 1950 on. With the removal of so many barriers to trade and finance, and with the fast rates of economic growth in most countries, the rates of increase of international trade were even faster than those of production. One may, of course, entertain the thought that trade might have increased still faster if exchange rates had varied less than they did, but this is hard to believe, what with annual rates of increase of 8 per cent and more over the years.

The years 1967 to 1969 were the years of the greatest convulsions of the exchange-rate structure. They comprised the devaluations of the pound sterling, the French franc, and a host of other currencies, and the upvaluation of the German mark. In addition, they were probably the years of the greatest uncertainty about exchange rates. Several crises of confidence led to forward rates with extraordinarily large discounts and premiums relative to the spot rates of several currencies. Yet, despite this record of devaluation, depreciation, and upvaluation and of a higher degree of uncertainty about the future of more currencies than the world had ever known, the volume of international trade in these three years showed the highest rates of increase in all recorded history. Trade increased by almost 12 per cent in 1968 and by 14 per cent in 1969. Would anybody dare to contend that trade would have increased even more if the exchange markets had been calm and the rates invariable in these years?

Lest someone suspect that the large increases in world trade were reflecting especially large increases in trade among countries with stable and unsuspected currencies, let us state that the trade of the countries of the European Economic Community increased in 1969 by 27 per cent among themselves, and their imports from the rest of the world increased by about 17 per cent. This was the year in which, after a severe crisis of confidence in the stability of their exchange values, the French franc was devalued by 12 per cent and the German mark, after a few weeks of unpegged rates, was upvalued by more than 9 per cent. If hereafter the advocates of fixed rates continue to propagate the theory that trade can flourish and grow only when exchange rates are held invariant and when traders and producers have full confidence in the invariance of these rates, we shall have to conclude that the creed of the believers is invariant and inflexible, no matter what goes on before their eyes and how much it contradicts their tenets.

The story of capital movements is not unlike that of trade. Foreign-exchange restrictions and prohibitions and controls of capital movements can be serious discouragements to foreign investment, but variations in exchange rates are not. The real impediments to capital movements are, in most cases, created by governments defending fixed exchange rates.

An Inducement to Speculation

The warnings that greater variability of exchange rates might discourage and impede international movements of capital funds have often been combined with warnings to the opposite effect, of inducement to excessive capital movements. The apparent contradiction is quickly resolved by adding that the supposed discouragement relates to long-term funds, whereas the supposed inducement refers to short-term or liquid funds. It is feared that flexible rates operate as an inducement to speculators who think they can anticipate changes in exchange rates and thereby make fat profits. Presumably it is not simply envy of the successful speculators that inspires the warnings, but rather fear that massive movements of speculative funds lead to unproductive uses of otherwise investible funds and to counterproductive changes in exchange rates—counterproductive because they misdirect the use of resources and the flow of goods and services. On a more technical level, the argument focuses on another implication: since the incentive to speculate on future changes of exchange rates can in most situations be effectively reduced or removed by an appropriate interest-rate policy—that is, by differentials between domestic and foreign interest rates—those who fear speculation in currencies have to show that greater flexibility of exchange rates would, because of the need for preventing excessive flows of speculative funds, impose costly restraints upon the monetary policy (interest-rate policy) of the monetary authorities.

It should be conceded that the problem of possibly "destabilizing" speculation, and of the resulting effects on exchange rates or interest rates or both, is not just a layman's bugbear; it has been raised by respected economists and seriously discussed in professional writings. Before we start examining it, however, we must settle the question of what is meant by destabilizing. If a currency is disaligned but maintained at its wrong peg by governmental restrictions and/or official interventions, and if speculators recognize that the official reserves are becoming depleted and the restrictions are not going to work effectively in the long run, the eventual onslaught of speculation, the mass exodus of liquid funds that may force the authorities to lower or remove the peg, is the result of *equilibrating* speculations. To call it destabilizing would be misuse of language. An honest use of "destabilizing" presupposes a warranted belief that the exchange rate which the speculators presume to be untenable is in fact well aligned and could without restrictions (and without any other measures that are not likely to be taken or to be effective) be maintained indefinitely, were it not for the transactions of "misguided" speculators.

Most of our practical experience with currency speculation has been under conditions of pegged exchange rates. Some people are inclined to argue that, if there can be so much speculation against pegged rates, how much more speculation could there be against variable rates! This is a crude fallacy because, if a speculator believes that the given exchange rate either undervalues or overvalues the currency, a rigidly pegged rate can be expected to be readjusted only in one direction, whereas a rate flexible within a band or with the possibility of a small crawl of the parity may change in either direction. Hence, the worst risk a wrongheaded speculator against a rigidly pegged rate is exposed to is that he will not make the profit he has hoped for; speculating against a more flexible rate, however, he actually loses if the rate moves in the unexpected direction. It should be obvious that riskless speculation is more attractive than speculation with a risk of loss: The inducement to speculation under a system of more flexible exchange rates is therefore smaller.

This argument, however, is not conclusive until it excludes or restricts the possibility that the greater risk to speculators under a system of greater rate flexibility is overcompensated by much more vivid expectations of rate changes. It might be argued that narrowly pegged rates create or reinforce the illusion of unchangeability, so that expectations of change are zero most of the time, whereas more flexible rates invite expectations of change all the time. It would follow that most of the time there would be *no* speculative flows of funds with narrowly pegged rates and *some* speculative flows with more flexible rates. However, what happens "most of the time" is not relevant to the issue in question; relevant is what happens in those situations in which the maintenance of the fixed parity is in doubt, that is, when the narrow pegging of an exchange rate has resulted in large changes in the reserves of the monetary authorities. In such situations the expected profits from speculating on a change become very much larger under a system of "fixed" rates; an abrupt and substantial change overnight or over a weekend is then expected, which could be offset only by a differential between national interest rates of several hundred per cent. (If one expects the price of foreign currency to be raised by 10 per cent within a week, only an interest rate of more than 520 per cent per annum would prevent speculators from buying huge amounts of foreign currency at today's price.) Under a system of greater flexibility such serious disalignments of exchange rates would never, or hardly ever, arise, and expectations of change would be confined to minuscule adjustments. Profits from small changes can be only small, inviting only moderate speculation, which can be easily discouraged, if this is wanted, by relatively minor differentials in interest rates.

For greater clarity we ought to separate the examination of the question of speculation according to the major types of greater flexibility of exchange rates. A widening of the band would do little to increase or reduce speculation if adjustments beyond the limits of the band were expected. The wider band is a device to cope with short-run changes of cyclical character. It has several merits. One of them is that it induces stabilizing speculation; it recruits private funds for the job, otherwise assigned to the monetary authorities, of taking a temporary excess supply of foreign currencies off the market and of meeting a temporary excess demand for foreign currencies. The official exchange-stabilization funds have to come into the market only if private funds are not adequate to do the job. Even more important is the fact that the wider band gives the authorities a chance to pursue fiscal and monetary policies that would otherwise be inoperative. Such policies presuppose that the rate of interest in the domestic economy can be moved to and kept at a level different from the rates prevailing abroad. Such differences cannot be maintained if the exchange rate is kept fixed within very narrow limits; if the exchange rate can be expected to return eventually from the edge of a wider band to its center, this variation is consistent with, and permits the maintenance of, a difference between domestic and foreign interest rates.

The device of the gliding parity is designed to cope with changes that are possibly of a long-run character, such as divergent trends in levels of costs and prices at home and abroad. A fixed parity will have to be adjusted eventually, and speculation will usually speed up this adjustment. But the customary policy of making this adjustment only as a last resort, and therefore with great delay and by substantial amounts, makes speculation riskless and highly profitable. If adjustment is made early and gradually, long before it is recognized as inevitable, speculation will be risky and not profitable. Moreover, it is easy to reduce any such expectations of profits by modest interest-rate differentials. For, if the crawl of the parity is by only a fraction of a per cent per week or per month, a tiny difference in the interest rate can offset the gain from the expected variation in the exchange rate. Should a central bank find it inexpedient to adapt the interest rate to the expected change in the exchange rate, it will have to accept the resulting increase or decrease in its foreign-exchange reserves; but it may confidently expect to see these changes in reserves reversed when its cumulative successive small adjustments in the parity have reached the equilibrium amount, that is, the magnitude required to make the exchange rate consistent with the cost-and-price levels at home and abroad that are attuned to a sustainable long-run flow of long-term capital funds.

All this sounds excessively theoretical and abstract. For those who are impressed more by historical evidence than by theoretical argument one may point to several chapters in the records of history.

During the 12 years of a floating exchange rate for the Canadian dollar, there were at no time any massive flows of speculative funds nor any substantial changes in the free exchange rate. Even the large periodic adjustments in exchange rates of the Brazilian cruzeiro, the Chilean escudo, and the Colombian peso in recent years have not resulted in much speculation since these countries adopted systems of frequent adjustments, commensurate with the rates of domestic price inflation. The large inflows of speculative funds into Germany (in 1968 and 1969) came to an immediate end as soon as the peg of the German mark was removed from its untenable position and the mark was allowed to float for a few weeks.

All known instances of heavy currency speculation related either to cases of fixed exchange rates or to cases of hyperinflation, where the exchange rates were adjusted too slowly or where the daily or weekly rate of adjustment was so large that no differential in interest rates could possibly match it.

Currency speculation is a function of disaligned exchange rates that are expected to undergo adjustment by large jumps. Systems of small and gradual adjustments of exchange rates reduce the likelihood of massive movements of speculative funds over national frontiers.

Misdirection through False Signals

Changes in prices—of goods, services, securities, and currencies —function as signals for the allocation and reallocation of productive resources. Most advocates of greater flexibility of foreign-exchange rates attach great importance to the real-adjustment function of changes in exchange rates. Opponents, however, fear that many of these changes may turn out to be momentary reflections of passing circumstances and that reallocations effected by the changes would prove unnecessary, undesirable, and wasteful. In other words, exchange rates in a market without stabilization fund, equalization account, or similar official buffer-stock arrangements would be overly sensitive and their variations would give false signals to the economy.

Similar complaints about false market signals have been raised, at all times and in all countries, with regard to a large variety of products, especially primary products. The arguments in favor of fixed prices, held constant by means of public intervention, are not always the same but they are often based on the same basic principles, for example, that a fall in the price of the product might lead to the destruction of productive facilities which would later have to be reconstructed at great cost when demand rises to its previous level. This is a popular argument also in support of support prices for currencies: If a temporary excess supply of foreign currency—say, as a result of an irregular, fluky inflow of capital—is allowed to reduce the price of foreign currency, many exporters may no longer be competitive in foreign markets and imported products may gain the customers previously served by domestic producers. Major reallocations of resources may be forced upon the unhappy producers of exportable goods and on those competing with imports. But, by the time the productive facilities have been adapted to the new situation, the excess supply and lower price of foreign currency may have disappeared and costly restoration of the previous capacities may be "commanded" by the market. The nation would have suffered a loss that could have been avoided had the exchange rate been maintained at its former level.

These warnings about an oversensitive signaling system and about oversensitive producer reactions to the signals emanating from that system are greatly exaggerated. Traders and producers are not any less aware of the possibility of false signals than are the warners who, in fear of false signals, advocate arrangements which eliminate all signals. To be sure, producers who choose to postpone reacting to lower proceeds incur losses in the hope of a return of favorable conditions. Maintenance of fixed exchange rates avoids these losses to producers, but only by socialization of the exchange risk. For, as the monetary authorities purchase the foreign currency supplied in excess, they undertake to carry the cost and the risk which otherwise would be borne by the producers in question. This shifting of the incidence of risks and other costs transfers the responsibility for decisions to persons who have no stake in the outcome and do not even know that there are any special costs involved.

Moreover, those who fear that foreign-exchange markets without official stabilization would be excessively sensitive to merely momentary changes in the flows of funds make some implicit assumptions which should be questioned. They either assume that there are no perceptive traders who can take advantage of small deviations from the rate that would balance the market over somewhat longer periods, or they believe that private parties cannot have the information and the judgment available to the officials in charge of market interventions.

There is no evidence of superior intelligence of official over private specialists in international finance. It may be a prejudice on my part, but I strongly incline to rate the insight and judgment of private specialists higher, at least in the most developed countries, and I do not see why they should not have access to the same information that is available to the officials. Of course, in some countries there may be no private traders able and willing to assume the risks of speculation stabilizing the exchange rates over periods long enough to avoid seasonal or other "dysfunctional" fluctuations. Their absence, however, is largely the result of the policy of the monetary authorities either prohibiting private speculation by various restrictions and controls or intervening constantly in the market so that there remains nothing for private traders to do but to act as agents or quasi-agents for the authorities. The heads of the control authorities may say that they have to intervene because there are not private traders to do the job, but in fact there are no traders because the officials have socialized and monopolized the trade.

What may be concluded from all these considerations? Where disturbances in the flows of funds through the foreign-exchange market are clearly temporary or reversible, provisions for greater flexibility of rates will not really result in rate variations, since private traders will do the same selling or buying operations that stabilization offices would do as official rate peggers. Where the disturbances are not clearly temporary or reversible, maintenance of fixed rates is not in the national interest. If certain variations of exchange rates suggests some drastic restructuring of the fixed capital used in production, the equipment for making products that can no longer be profitably produced at the changed exchange rates will hardly be scrapped in such haste that the owners will deplore the "wanton" destruction in case of a reversal of the rate change. The story about capital equipment having been scrapped in obedience to market signals and later replaced at high cost after the signals proved false is a tale told to secure postponement of structural adjustments; history provides no empirical evidence indicating that such premature scrapping has ever occurred.

The fear of large social losses through false signals from an exchange market with more flexible rates is not justified.

Lack of Good Indicators for Small Changes

When an exchange rate is badly disaligned, it may not be clear what magnitude of adjustment would be required to realign it, but there will be no doubt about the direction in which it should be changed. Can this be said about a small disalignment? The doubt suggested in this question may appear to be the strongest argument against the frequent small adjustments that would be made under some systems of greater flexibility of exchange rates.

A widening of the band of permissible variations of rates around a fixed par value of exchange would not be faulted by the apparent lack of good indicators for decisions on small changes. Especially where the monetary authorities refrain from intervening aggressively in the market, there is no need for any precise indicators of desirable action. If the authorities do not try either to push up the exchange rate or to pull it down by their operations in the market, but merely defend the rate, merely try to hold it within the band by selling foreign currency at or near the upper limit or buying at or near the lower edge of the band, they need no gauges, registers, or any other clues to tell them what to do and when. (A change in the Fund Articles of Agreement permitting a wider band around par value might discourage or prohibit official purchases of foreign currency at high prices and official sales at low prices. In any case, self-restraining ordinances to this effect by the authorities of member countries taking advantage of a wider-band provision would be appropriate.)

Greater flexibility of the crawling-peg variety would need indicators telling in which direction the peg should be moved. This is so by definition regarding the formula-determined crawl. But, as I have said several times, no satisfactory formula has been found and none is likely to be found. Indicators of the direction of adjustment would be needed also for discretionary, negotiated, or agreed changes of parity. (Some central bankers think of the crawling peg always as parity changes directed by a formula; this is a mistake, since the proponents of the crawling peg, or gliding parity, have included discretionary adjustments as a possible operating mode of their schemes.) Finally, directional indicators would be needed if countries decide under the present rules of the Fund to readjust the parities of their currencies more frequently and by smaller percentages than has been done during the first 25 years of the International Monetary Fund.

In the last case, of greater flexibility under the present Articles of Agreement, it would be a little odd to plead "fundamental disequilibrium" in order to justify an adjustment of the parity by 1 per cent or less (or, for that matter, by even 2 or 3 per cent). The correct explanation of such a move would be an "incipient disequilibrium," something for which the Bretton Woods Agreements did not provide. One may presume, however, that the Executive Directors of the Fund would accept such a justification as appropriate, as an "incipient fundamental disequilibrium," so to speak. Of course, the problem of conformance with the Articles and their legal interpretation is very different from the problem with which we are concerned, namely, how one can be sure that the par value of a currency had better be moved in one direction rather than in the other when no serious disalignment can be diagnosed.

An answer may be suggested by the analogy of an adjustment of bank rate, the discount rate of the central bank. Central bankers seldom have grave doubts about the direction in which they ought to change the discount rate, even when they have no index and no indicator telling them whether the change should be ¼, ½, 1, or 1½ per cent. When the portfolio of domestic assets of the central bank has been growing at a fast rate, when the supply of money and near-money has been increasing fast, when business is booming and prices are rising, and when the demand for credit is strong, the authorities will hardly consider lowering the official discount rate; they will only think of raising it. Similarly, when the foreign reserves of the central bank have been declining steadily, when the spot prices of foreign currencies have been close to the upper edge of the band around parity, and forward rates likewise or even higher, and when imports have been increasing more than exports, the authorities would hardly consider raising the par value of their currency, but they might well think of lowering it.

This does not mean that the few criteria just mentioned ought to be regarded as the only or most reliable indicators of proper parity adjustment. It may well be that they give a "bum steer," a wrong directive, to the authorities. But if the adjustment is by no more than, say, one-half of 1 per cent per quarter year, not much harm can be done, and the move can be reversed within a few weeks or months. On the other hand, if the situation persists and reserves and exchange rates continue in the same stance, the move may be repeated after three months (or earlier by a smaller percentage change).

Thus, that one cannot with any great confidence assert that the currency is overvalued or undervalued by 1 or 2 per cent does not mean that one cannot recommend or prescribe with good conscience a downward or upward adjustment of its par value by 1 or 2 per cent, or preferably by only one-half of 1 per cent per quarter, to be repeated or reversed according to circumstances.

Perhaps it should be made clear that very small parity adjustments, say, by 1/26 of 1 per cent a week or by 1/12 of 1 per cent a month, need not affect the exchange rate prevailing in the market at the time, provided the rate is within a widened band and not too close to one of the edges of the band. Assume that the band of permissible variations of the spot rate is 2 per cent up or down from parity and that the spot rate at the moment is 1½ per cent below parity (that is, the price of foreign currency is 1½ per cent above parity). If now the par value is reduced by 1/12 of one per cent, the spot rate is within the new as well as the former band, and need not change at all; indeed, the authorities may by some sales of foreign exchange prevent it from changing. The unchanged rate will then be a little closer to the new parity and a little further away from the edge of the band. If afterwards reserves continue to decline and/or the exchange rate tends to go lower, the authorities will repeat the action. The sum of the consecutive parity adjustments will eventually be reflected in the actual exchange rate, even if no single adjustment of the parity affects the exchange rate at which transactions take place in the market at the time of the move.

All this applies only to the case of a currency that is not seriously disaligned. We have been discussing the question of greater flexibility to cope with incipient disalignments. The case of serious disalignment was discussed earlier and there the high cost of deferring adjustment was emphasized. Thus, it was implied that frequent small changes of exchange rates are not recommended as a remedy for serious disalignment.

The two cases have something in common: The authorities deciding on the change in par value may make mistakes. In the case of a large disalignment of exchange rates, the mistake will hardly ever be in the direction of change, but rather in its magnitude; in the case of an incipient, not clearly perceptible disalignment, the mistake may be in the direction of change, never in its magnitude. However, there is little harm in a small change—say, 1/12 or even ½ of one per cent—in the wrong direction, whereas there may be substantial harm in an excessively large change, say, by 12 per cent if only 8 per cent would have been required. That in cases of serious disalignment we can trust the indicators regarding the right direction of adjustment while we cannot trust them in decisions about the small adjustments recommended by the advocates of greater flexibility is a poor, indeed a silly, arguement against flexibility. The disturbances caused by large exchange-rate adjustments of inappropriate magnitude are very much more serious than any disturbances that could be caused by a trivially small and easily reversible adjustment.

Jumping, Trotting, and Crawling Pegs

In concluding this discussion let us recall that it has dealt with objections to greater flexibility and, therefore, indirectly with the comparative effects of abrupt as contrasted with gradual adjustments of exchange rates. Five arguments in favor of infrequent and large changes in opposition to frequent and small changes have been examined: that greater flexibility invites financial intemperance, that it may lead to competitive devaluations, that it discourages foreign trade and investment, that it is likely to cause more economic waste because of false signals to producers, and that it will often result in mistaken decisions because of the lack of good indicators. All these arguments have been found wanting. Unless other arguments against greater flexibility are produced and found valid, the opposition cannot be sustained.

Let us recall also that this has not been a comparison between unalterable and flexible rates. Such a comparison would make little sense if it had to be relevant for countries with separate central banks and monetary and fiscal autonomy. Such countries will always be subject to forces operating to disalign the exchange rates of their currencies vis-à-vis other currencies. Since realignment through corrective policies or through aggregate-demand adjustment is excessively costly, exchange-rate adjustment is the only rational technique of restoring balance. Thus, the choice is between the infrequent but large changes and small but frequent changes of the exchange rate.

Some countries do not even have this choice: where the rate of demand and price inflation is much larger than the average inflation rate of the world, frequent *and* large devaluations will be required. Countries with "trotting inflations" cannot postpone devaluation for very long and cannot do with small percentages of devaluation unless they devalue every few days. If, for example, domestic prices rise by 100 per cent per year, the prices of foreign moneys have to be raised at a similar speed, that is, by 1¼ per cent per week, 6 per cent per month, or almost 20 per cent per quarter. With an inflation rate of 50 per cent per year, the commensurate increases in prices of foreign currency are over ¾ per cent per week, 3½ per cent per month, or 11 per cent per quarter. These are not small rates of devaluation, certainly not if quarterly intervals are chosen; yet the term "jumping peg" would not be fitting, since "jump" in this context connotes a sudden, abrupt change after a long delay. The term "crawling peg" would fit even less, since the maximum speed for a "crawl" has been defined as 3 per cent a year. Thus, it is a "trotting peg" that corresponds to a trotting inflation. Several Latin-American countries—Chile, Brazil, Colombia—have used this system.

The chief difference between the systems of jumping and crawling pegs lies in the underlying official attitude: under the former, the change in the exchange rate is regarded as a means of last resort, undertaken only after long hesitation and delay, usually after all sorts of corrective measures restricting the flows of goods, services, and capital funds have proved unsuccessful. The delay is costly and the restrictive measures may be detrimental. To avoid delay and restrictions, a system of frequent and small adjustments of the exchange rate is recommended. If the governments had been using the provisions of the Fund Agreement without undue delays and without restrictions of trade and finance it would never have been necessary to invent and propose any fancy schemes, like crawling pegs and movable bands. It is conceivable that the men heading the monetary authorities of financially developed countries continue to resist the adoption of such schemes but stop resisting the prescription of prompt realignments of exchange rates. In this case the world might get greater flexibility of exchange rates without changing the formal rules of the game. Still, "conceivable" is not the same as "likely," and those who understand the economic consequences of delays and restrictions should therefore not relax in their efforts to open the minds of the conscientious objectors to reform.

OPPOSITION TO FLOATING RATES

Traditionalists among practitioners—if I may assume that the class of nontraditional practitioners is not a null-class—resist all proposed changes in exchange rates, vehemently object to all proposals of greater flexibility of exchange rates, and passionately oppose proposals for floating exchange rates. The three degrees of disapprobation can be well understood: A change every few years is bad enough to be fought as long as possible; change every few months is quite unacceptable and all powers of dissuasion must be used to avert the adoption of such schemes; but the possibility of change every day is so preposterous, anarchic, conducive to chaos, that it must be condemned as downright "impractical," by which the practitioner means that no arguments are needed to show why.

Keynes believed in the power of ideas but he knew that each generation of practitioners and politicians is influenced by the ideas they learned in their youth. The time lag is sometimes shorter than thirty years, but I do not think that the time for acceptance of the idea of freely floating exchange rates as an enduring system has come. It is futile to try now to sell this idea to the men in power or the men of influence.

It is something else, however, to recommend floating rates for a limited period of transition between the unpegging of a hopelessly disaligned rate and its repegging at a different, more appropriate level. There is opposition to this proposal too, but it should be possible to overcome it by reasoned argument.

Motion, Actual and Potential

Most of the adjectives used in connection with exchange-rate systems have connotations of motion, actual or potential. The words "fixed," "pegged," and "floating" refer to potential motion; the first two participles are meant to convey the idea that potential movements of the exchange rate are being prevented by official actions of the authorities, whereas the third participle is to tell us that potential movements are not being prevented and that the exchange rate is allowed to go wherever the forces of the free market may move it.

The verbs "jumping," "trotting," "crawling," and "gliding" are used to modify the nouns peg, parity, or par value and refer to the abruptness of gradualness, and speed of movement. They are all intransitive verbs, which may be somewhat misleading by suggesting that the predicted motions are not the result of actions by others. Pegs or parities do not jump, trot, or crawl by themselves, but instead are moved by actions taken by others. Most users of these words do not mind, and most of the listeners do not take the time to be seriously confused by such semantic antics.

In the following discussions we shall no longer be concerned with the jump or the crawl imposed on peg or parity, but rather with the removal of a peg and the cessation of official selling or buying of foreign exchange for the purpose of keeping their rates from moving. Thus, rates will be affected chiefly by nonofficial bids and offers and will be allowed to "float" with the waves of the free market until a new intervention level (peg) is determined, presumably on the basis of the experience gained during the period of abstention from official rate-pegging.

Three Kinds of Floating Rates

We distinguish three kinds of floating exchange rates. One is the pure type, genuinely floating rates where monetary authorities do absolutely no selling or buying of foreign exchange. The other two types permit of some selling or buying by the authorities, provided that these transactions are not designed to keep exchange rates at some predetermined level. What purposes may official transactions in the exchange market serve if we are still to find the designation of floating rates legitimate? There is the Canadian type and there is the German type of floating rates, and they can be easily characterized.

Sales or purchases of U.S. dollars by the Canadian authorities were designed to smoothen the fluctuations in the market without, however, preventing rates from following any trend that might have been dictated by changes in nonofficial supply and demand. To smoothen fluctuations but not to interfere with a trend is a task that cannot be carried out literally but can be approached by a simple rule of thumb: not to allow the working balance of the intervention currency to be reduced or increased beyond some stated limits, limits which allow only relatively modest changes in reserves. If only a small amount of reserves may be made available for meeting a sudden excess demand for foreign exchange, and if only a small portion of it can be used per day, a rise in the price of the U.S. dollar (that is, a depreciation of the Canadian dollar) can at best be slowed down but cannot be prevented. Obversely, if foreign reserves are not allowed to be increased but by a small amount, and only by a portion of this per day, not all of an emerging excess supply of foreign exchange can be acquired by the monetary authorities, and the price reduction of the U.S. dollar (that is, an appreciation of the Canadian dollar) can at best be slowed down but cannot be prevented. This system was used in Canada from 1950 to 1959. (In the last years of that period of seemingly floating rates, 1959 to 1962, official purchases of U.S. dollars assumed dimensions which suggest an intention to lower the external value of the Canadian dollar.)

When Germany unpegged the German mark in September 1969, the central bank did not refrain from intervening in the exchange market; it started to unload some of the huge dollar reserves it had piled up during the period in which it had kept the mark undervalued. The mark would have appreciated (that is, the rate of the dollar would have declined) in any case after the official purchases of dollars were stopped; but the official sales of dollars from the swollen reserves undoubtedly hastened the appreciation of the mark. One may attribute the dollar sales to a design to raise the external value of the mark—in order to correct its undervaluation—or to a design to dispose of the unwanted plethora of reserves. The first of these interpretations of the official interventions would militate against recognizing the period between unpegging and repegging as one of floating rates: managed rates are not floating rates. The second interpretation, however, would still permit the use of the designation of floating rates. The intention to reduce excessive reserves (or to add to inadequate reserves) may justify official sales (or purchases) in the exchange market without inviting the charge that the authorities are attempting to manage the rates.

To take intentions and motivations as criteria of definitions is admittedly not very satisfactory, and I would understand a theorist's refusal to recognize these impure types as floating rates. On the other hand, things are pure and perfect only in our abstract conceptual schemes, never in reality. From this point of view, I think our analysis will not be excessively polluted by some largess in labeling real institutions and arrangements with designations more appropriate for ideal types.

Periods of Floating Rates

The realignment of exchange rates which have been disaligned for a long time can never be a precision job; it is usually a hit-or-miss business based on impressionistic guesses and hunches. Experts will come up with widely diverging recommendations: While one group may propose a devaluation of 15 per cent, another will assert that nothing less than 60 per cent would do, and there will be advisors in favor of virtually every point between.

Under conditions usually prevailing in countries in which disaligned exchange rates have long been maintained, it is advisable to allow a period of floating rates before a new peg or parity is chosen. Not that one could expect the "correct" rate to emerge from the free play of the market. In the first few months after the unpegging, the docket of short-term claims and liabilities built up by the leads and lags that developed in anticipation of an exchange-rate alteration has to be worked down; and most of the time rumors and guesses of the new par value to be established may induce speculative capital flows that will be reversed later. Still, a sufficiently long period of floating rates may provide information that could not be obtained otherwise.

There are other arguments against prompt repegging. If the currency has been overvalued, the removal of the peg will allow the prices of foreign currencies to rise with consequent increases in the prices of imported goods and of exportables. Organized labor will demand wage increases, and employers may be ready to meet these demands. It is, in most situations, poor strategy to fix a new par value for the currency before it is known how much domestic labor a unit of currency can buy. This is not much different in instances where the currency has been undervalued. Although prices of imports and of exportables will in this case be lowered when the peg is removed, the imported inflation caused by the previous undervaluation of the currency may not yet have worked itself out; the "demand pull" may still be operating in the markets, including the labor market. Again, it will be prudent not to fix the new parity prematurely, but rather to wait until things have settled down.

Different indicators and different sectoral interests often call for very different levels of the new peg. In such situations it would be most unwise, from political as well as economic points of view, to hasten a decision, which cannot help being partial to some interests. If the authorities, instead, let the exchange rate float, they escape the charge of partiality, especially if they refrain from all interventions in the market and let anonymous forces determine the movements of the rate.

Some practitioners warn against the uncertainty that prevails during such periods of floating rates, and they assert that it invites inordinate movements of speculative capital funds. The factual evidence supports precisely the opposite view. As was pointed out above, speculative movements are maximized when rates are maintained by official pegs at levels that are considered untenable; and this is true of old parities that have become disaligned and of new parities that are not credible. Speculation is rampant just before pegs are removed and again after pegs are reset at levels which the market judges to be wrong. There is strong evidence for the proposition that speculation dies down as soon as a misplaced peg is removed, and does not revive until the establishment of a new parity is rumored.

CONCLUSION

There is danger and waste in premature action taken in haste with insufficient deliberation. No evidence, however, indicates or even suggests that any government in the last 25 years has acted rashly in adjusting the exchange rate of its currency. In the majority of instances the adjustments came after long delays, sometimes several years late, and the delays caused heavy economic damage.

A large part of this lecture was devoted to an examination of the general reasons for such delays. We first looked into the causes of political resistance to adjustments in exchange rates. Not all of the resistance was without economic merit; some of it was based on serious economic considerations; but eventually and on balance the arguments were found not to be sustainable. The strongest reason for postponing adjustment has probably been the realization that nobody could know exactly (or even approximately) how much of a change in the exchange rate would be needed to realign it. The fear that any magnitude chosen may be far from "right" is not unwarranted. However, if adjustments were more frequent and by smaller amounts, the risk of grave mistakes would be drastically reduced. The smaller risk of wrong decisions and the avoidance of costly delays are two very important points in favor of arrangements that facilitate greater flexibility of exchange rates.

Confronted with many strong objections which men in financial circles and central banks have raised against greater flexibility of exchange rates, we embarked on an examination of their arguments. We have found most of them unconvincing, and some of them untenable. No matter whether any of the specific schemes for greater flexibility that have been under discussion in recent years will finally be adopted or whether any other arrangements will eventually find favor among the men in charge, there is little doubt that in the future exchange-rate adjustments should and will be made more frequently and by smaller amounts. The system of rigid rates pegged for years at wrong levels and supported by selective restrictions and bureaucratic controls of trade, payments, and capital movements, is thoroughly discredited. (This system was *not* what the signers of the Bretton Woods Agreements intended.)

Still, even if enlightened governments eventually agree that greater flexibility of exchange rates would be a good thing for world trade and capital movements, there will always be some countries entering the era of more frequent and *small* adjustments with the exchange rate of their own currency so badly out of line that they will not be spared the agony of deciding on a *big* adjustment. In addition, countries with neatly aligned exchange rates may at any time be thrown off balance by some extra-large cost push reducing their competitiveness in international trade, and they may not be able to restore balance by small exchange-rate adjustments. Thus, some countries will be faced with all the problems of resistance, delay, distortion, waste, speculation, and political conflict that are associated with large "fundamental disequilibrium." For these countries a period of freely floating exchange rates, perhaps mitigated by neutral, Canadian-type interventions, will in most cases be advisable. Let us remember that the uncertainty created by unpegged exchange rates is almost always smaller and far less harmful than the uncertainty that stems from incorrectly pegged exchange rates.

NOTE

1. *Currency Devaluation in Developing Countries,* Essays in International Finance, No. 86 (Princeton: Princeton University International Finance Section, June 1971).

ABOUT THE AUTHOR

FRITZ MACHLUP is Walker Professor of Economics and International Finance, Emeritus, at Princeton University. From 1935 to 1947 he was Goodyear Professor of Economics at the University of Buffalo, and from 1947 to 1960 Hutzler Professor of Political Economy at the Johns Hopkins University. He is currently Professor of Economics at New York University.

He is the author of more than fifteen books and over a hundred articles in learned journals. His works have appeared in French, German, Italian, Japanese, Spanish, and Russian translations. Some recent books are *Essays in Economic Semantics, Remaking the International Monetary System,* and *Education and Economic Growth.*

Professor Machlup has served as president of the Southern Economic Association, the American Economic Association, and the American Association of University Professors. He is currently President of the International Economic Association.